Other boo

Hon

F
Fre...ch Flea Bites
French Cricket
French Kisses
French Lessons
French Impressions: Brittany
French Impressions: The Loire Valley
French Impressions: The Dordogne River
French Impressions: Lower Normandy
150 Fabulous French Recipes
The Brittany Blogs
Home & Dry in Normandy (compilation)
French Kisses (compilation)
Love Letters to France
France and the French
A Balkan Summer
A Year Behind Bars
How to write a Best-Seller
The Naked Truth about Women
The Naked Truth about Dieting

and the Jack Mowgley Mysteries

Death Duty
Deadly Tide
Dead Money
Death á la Carte
Dead & Buried

LA PUCE PUBLICATIONS
e-mail: lapucepublications@hotmail.co.uk.
website: www.george-east.net

I've been avoiding writing this book for thirty years.

That's a record, even for me.

I finally capitulated when my wife pointed out that I was cutting it more than a bit fine. It was time to get on with it before I, along with mudlarking, trolley buses, bombsites and jiving the night away at The Savoy am naught but dust and distant memory.

She was as ever right, but you will understand my reluctance to get started. Such a responsibility to get it right, and so many opportunities to get it wrong. Apart from the factual and statistical cock-ups, what about the stuff that I simply disremember? I take comfort that those with better memories will put me right in time for the next edition...and the subsequent volumes.

But here's the really important bit: This book is not so much about me as about our historic, heroic and often hard-done-by home city, and what it was like to grow up here at a particular time in its long history. I will hopefully be seen as no more than the conduit to times and places and attitudes and ways of life long gone. Yes, these are my experiences, but they're also the experiences of tens of thousands of people who grew up in Pompey immediately after the Second World War. And, of course, they are experiences and memories shared by all those who grew up at that time in towns and cities across the land.

For my contemporaneous Portmuthians, I hope this jumble of anecdotes and misty memories will remind them of a time when summers were endless and always sunny, and life sometimes hard but mostly carefree. Younger readers will hopefully get an inkling of what real life was like less than a lifetime ago and just how cushdy* they have it nowadays.

The past is said to be like a foreign country, but to many young Portmuthians I suspect this account will seem to be more about a place and time many light years away.

P.S. For me there's a particular resonance to the title of this collection of anecdotes, unreliable recollections and confessions.

Just before leaving us, our father made my brother and I promise he would spend eternity lying side-by-side with his wife of more than sixty years. He would leave it to my brother and I as to what we chose to say about him at the funeral, but he would like to be remembered as 'Just a Pompey Boy'. Given that he and so many others were born elsewhere but came to see themselves as true sons and daughters of the city, I think that proves how Portsmouth takes new citizens to her heart and finds a place in theirs.

*'Cushdy' is an old Romany word for 'easy' or 'good', and a fine example of how Portsmouth argot and slang have adopted and stolen so many words and expressions from other languages and dialects.

On a technical note, credit has been given to the authors or owners of all photographs (if known).

Before we begin, a confession.

Although I grew up in and can trace my ancestors back to the 18th century in the city, if you wanted to be lairy (now there's a proper Pompey word) you could claim I am not technically a true Portmuthian. I was conceived there, but born next door in Hayling Island.

It was late 1943 and my mother and father and brother John lived not far from the Dockyard. Unsurprisingly the Royal Navy's premier base was a magnet for the Luftwaffe. It also has to be remembered that bombing was in those days literally a hit-or-miss affair, and we were very much in the catchment area bound to suffer from what they now call collateral damage.

My dad was a fire warden, and when my mum became heavy with me he moved her and John across the water to what he thought would be the safety of Hayling Island. What he didn't know was that the authorities did their best to entice the Luftwaffe to unload their deadly cargoes there rather than on Pompey. A good example of how effective were the fires, fake military buildings and other decoys is that on the night of April 17th, 1941, ninety percent of the bombs intended for the Portsmouth Dockyard fell instead on Hayling Island. Thankfully, it is reported that casualties were light.

According to my mother, there was another big raid on the night of my birth.

My dad had been practicing wetting the baby's head at the nearby Olive Leaf pub, and when news came that I had put in an early appearance he invited the regulars back to meet me. According to Mother, dad and the guests rolled a cask of ale back to toast my health on the premises, though being full of hops it would have been virtually undrinkable. I think there's an early clue to my dad's character there. Full of heart, good intentions and ideas, but not all of them thought properly through.

Anyway, I think it true to say I entered the world at a time of noise and fire and danger. My mother often said that my dramatic arrival was the reason I was always such a handful. She was not usually one to hold grudges, but never forgave Air Marshal Goering for a near-miss which totalled our greenhouse and damaged the midwife's bicycle beyond repair.

P.S. I can find no record of any bombs falling on Hayling Island on January 31st, 1944. For sure, my dear mother certainly had a gift for invention and had the most elastic of imaginations. A typical example was her claim that a very poor copy of Vincent Van Gogh's Sunflowers hanging in the passage was a preparatory work by the great man himself. When I pointed out that the flowers were all blue, she said it was a well-known fact that Mr Van Gogh had suffered from sporadic colour-blindness as well as depression.

Mother also claimed that her great-great-great-great-grandfather had been at Nelson's side in the Battle of Trafalgar. And that it was probably him and not Captain Hardy who kissed the hero farewell on his deathbed. She also knew from family stories that it had been her ancestor who had helped lower the corpse of the great man into the cask of brandy which would keep him fresh for the long journey home. Perhaps, as my wife believes, this endearing trait of my dear mother for invention and exaggeration was what made me such a compulsive tale-teller.

Little angel: A poser even at three, and with big brother John

Memory is a funny thing, or at least mine is.

I don't know about you, but I don't have any new ones about times past. What I mean by that is that all my memories are the same, familiar recollections, with no sudden recalls of a previously forgotten event or experience. No amount of memory-jogging by people who claim to have shared an episode of my life can restore them. They are all filed away, and dredged up when talking or writing or thinking about the past. But new ones never seem to surface. Perhaps my memory banks are like a computer with only a limited amount of space on the hard drive. Perhaps in the way that people undergo cognitive therapy, writing this book will reveal sudden flashes of events as yet locked away in the dark place of unrecalled times. If that happens, I'll let you know.

Another disappointment is how relatively late my memories begin. I know people who claim to recall laying in their prams. Others casually say they can remember being in the womb, or even recall events from a previous life. The best I can do is from the age of five, and I also have great holes in the membrane of my recall of events in much later years. This is a bitter disappointment, especially if a fraction of the tales told about and to me are remotely true.

Some years ago in an on-line forum, an old friend (who I can't actually call to mind) reminded me of the time he saw me standing on a table in the bar at South Parade Pier. I was, he said, drinking Babycham from a Pompey girl's shoe. It wasn't working too well, he said, as the white stiletto-heel was made up mostly of straps and a hole where the toe went. Another detail he mentioned was that I was completely naked except for my socks.

According to him, he and a chum got me dressed and to my then home in St Edward's Road in Southsea, where they propped me up on the threshold and rang the bell. When the door opened, they said, I fell forward, slurred 'Hello mother' and embraced the hatstand before collapsing on the passageway floor. If the story is true, how can it be that I have absolutely no recall of this event, even when reminded in detail of it? Was it embarrassment at the thought of such activity that wiped the memory from my hard drive? Or was it that such bacchanalian indulgences in my youth were so common that such a mild example was not considered worth retaining?

Apart from the disappointment of not having access to so much of my past life, I worry that there may be whole chunks that are lost forever. What if I was once an undercover MI5 agent masquerading as a pipe fitter and welder? Or a still-unexposed serial killer?

The worst thing about these gaps is that, at the end of our days, memories are all we have left, and I seem to have lost so many of them.

1949

George Orwell's dystopian novel 1984 is published. The first passenger jet plane makes its maiden flight and the Soviet Union tests its first atomic bomb. Popular recordings on USA Billboard include Lucky Old Sun by Frankie Lane, Far Away Places by Bing Crosby and Buttons and Bows by Dinah Shore. Nearer to home, Portsmouth Football Club celebrates its Golden Jubilee by winning the First Division League Championship and registering a record attendance of 51,385. Ventriloquist's dummy and radio star Archie Andrews appears at the Theatre Royal, and Geraldo and his Full Broadcasting Orchestra perform at The Savoy Ballroom. A small boy called George starts school at Cottage Grove Primary.

This is my first memory; unlike so many others, it stays as sharp and colourful as an old movie which has been digitally enhanced. I can also see the event not only through my eyes but from another person's point of view; it is as if for that brief moment I am a spectator as well as the subject.

It is morning, and I am sobbing and gasping for breath. Tears course down my cheeks and mingle with the snot from my streaming nose. I can feel the stern grasp of my mother's hand and the unfriendly cobbles through the soles of my sandals as I am dragged along.

To my right is a vision from Hell. The old stable doors lie open and the otherwise gloomy interior is made lighter than day by roaring flame and flying sparks. There is the sound of metal clanging against metal, and the nose-fizzingly rank odour of burning coals, seared hoofs and horse and human sweat.

On the other side of Smith's Lane lies the cause of my distress. It is my first day at school, and my mother has been forced to drag me to Cottage Grove.

Ironically, the tears and snot flow again when she comes to collect me. Not because I still feel a sense of betrayal that she abandoned me here, but because she wants to take me home.

~

I made a sentimental visit to Cottage Grove School half a century after leaving, and my first reaction was how small everything seemed. What I remembered as lofty, steepled roofs and soaring railings looked so much smaller and less intimidating to my grown-up perspective. But it was uplifting to see that, outside at any rate, so little had changed. In an area of Portsmouth where whole streets of shops and houses had to be born again after the bombing, my old school was comfortingly familiar. There were the same Victorian-era, solid church hall-type buildings of flint and weathered brick, with the caretaker 'Jack' Frost's cottage (or lair as we liked to think of it) guarding the gate. For a moment, I wondered if his shade might be lurking inside still, and would come out to shout at me for drawing a chalk wicket on the playground wall or a willy in the toilet.

Also missing was Mr Burn's giant sit-up-and-beg boneshaker black bicycle, which should have been leaning against the railings beneath the elm tree by the main gate. Another change was that Smith's Lane sadly no longer lived up to its name. To be fair, I suppose there's not much call for horse shoe-ing in modern-day Portsmouth.

A particularly reassuringly unchanged feature was the asphalt playground, place of delight and dismay, blood and tears and games like Tag, British Bulldog, Roundheads and Cavaliers. And the brief burning of the flame lit by my first true love.

Before I turned to go, I shut my eyes and the buzz and roar and hullaballoo of the modern world faded. For a few precious seconds I found myself back in a time of innocence and simple emotions that we must all leave behind.

~

To the best of my recollection, Sheila Parker (name changed lest the real person take offence or disagree with my memories of her) was one of twins, and a pretty girl with a blonde page-boy hairstyle held in place by plastic butterfly clips. I seem to remember a sprinkling of freckles across her dinky snub nose. She wore a pair of NHS spectacles, one lens of which was covered with strips of pink Elastoplast. This was a common treatment for what was then known as a 'lazy eye', which for some reason was a not uncommon childhood ailment in those days. I don't know what it says about me, but in later life I was to have relationships with several otherwise attractive girls with squints or, in two cases, a glass eye.

Shelia's patch didn't put me off, and indeed added a sort of mystique to her appearance. It wouldn't be true to say it was love at first sight, as I can't recall when the bolt struck. But I do remember pledging my eternal love by placing on her finger a plastic ring I think I found in a Jamboree Bag. Or perhaps it came as a free gift in a comic or a packet of breakfast cereal.

At that age and time, the options for courtship were pretty limited and our love manifested itself mainly in walking hand-in-hand and round and round the playground at every break time. We were the centre of interest for the week our undying love lived, mostly of course from the girls. The boys thought I had lost my mind, which in a way I had, but no remarks were made in my hearing as I was already big for my age. For sure, losing my heart deeply but briefly was a sign of things to come.

What more could a boy want? On Southsea prom at around four years of age. Note the pudding basin cut and the blue, knitted bathers. When wet they took on several pounds of seawater and ended up round the ankles.

A Brief History

There is no mention of Portsmouth in the Domesday Book, but some areas which would become part of the town are to be found there. Mind you, some of the dodgier areas look as if they haven't had a wash-and-brush-up since those times.

Around then (the late 11th Century) there were no more than a couple of hundred people scraping a living in and around the island. Salty marshlands and frequent inundations were not hospitable to agriculture, and it wasn't an immediately obvious setting for a port. They were usually good judges of where to set up shop, but nobody seems to know why the Romans invested so heavily in establishing a settlement at Portchester.

The development of the town and port was gradual and involved a number of monarchs. Henry the First saw the potential as he passed through on route to Normandy in 1114, and it was he who built the castle on the site of the old Roman settlement at Portchester. In 1194 (allegedly after a good day's hunting at Boarhunt) Richard The Lionheart granted Portsmouth a Royal Charter. This was an important step for the town as it granted the citizens certain rights, including holding a weekly market and exemption from certain taxes.

Spool on to the 13th century, and, though with a population of no more than a thousand, Portsmouth was becoming recognised as a significant port.

Exports included wool and grain; imports were wine, woad for use as a dye, iron, and wax for candles.

One of the major problems for peaceful trading was the almost continuous battles with the French: Portsmouth was constantly raided, and burned down four times during the 14th century. The endless aggro led to fortifications at the entry to the port, like the Round Tower, ordered by Henry V. In 1494, Henry VII added the Square Tower and the destiny of Portsmouth was set in place when the king commanded the formation of the dockyard.

Southsea Castle appeared in the 16th century, and on a blustery July day in 1545 Henry VIII stood on its walls and watched in horror as his flagship *Mary Rose* sank with all hands during a skirmish with a French fleet.

By the start of the 17th century, the population of Portsmouth had grown to 2000 and wealthy burghers began building houses in what we now call Old Portsmouth. By the end of the century there was a taste of what was to come when the town was said to have reached 'bursting point'.

Come the 18th century and things were really happening. In 1764 a body of men called the Improvement Commissioners was set up in Portsea and had the power to pave and clean the streets. They also appointed a man called a Scavenger who collected rubbish with a cart, once a week. Some of today's citizens claim the service has gone downhill since then. In 1776 the town fathers were given authority to light the streets with oil lamps, and from 1783 they appointed night watchmen to patrol them.

The town was really put on the map in 1805, when Admiral Lord Nelson sallied out to the Battle of Trafalgar on HMS Victory - with my maternal ancestor on board if you believe Mother's claim.

The town grew apace off the island over the next two centuries, and was granted City status in 1926. By 1939 the population of Portsmouth stood at 260,000 and has more or less remained at that figure.

It has been a long and often dramatic journey, but all the turbulent events have melded into the fabric of what makes Portsmouth a very special city.

1952

Tea rationing ends, Great Britain explodes its first atom bomb and Sooty the glove puppet makes his debut on TV. The British pop charts are launched, and include 'Wheel of Fortune' by Kay Starr, 'Cry' by Johnny Ray and the Four Lads, and 'Auf Weiderseh'n Sweetheart' by Vera Lynn. Locally, Billy Cotton and His Band Show, Anne Shelton and Semprini appear at Portsmouth's Theatre Royal. Ted Heath and his band perform at the Savoy, and Ivy Benson and her All Girl Orchestra are on the stage at the Embassy Theatre. Portsmouth accordionist Chiz Bishop (17) of Beecham Road regains the All-Britain Amateur Solo Piano-Accordionist Championship. The nation and Empire mourn the passing of His Royal Majesty King George VI, but welcome the new monarch, Queen Elizabeth II.

Times were changing, even at Cottage Grove Primary School.

Having said that, the teaching principles, attitudes and physical structures (including the toilets) seemed not that different from when the school had been built in the tail end of the Victorian era. That and how we lived then are probably reasons why I, born in the middle of the 20th century, feel spiritually closer to the previous one.

Laid out in serried ranks on the highly-polished herring-bone block wooden floors of the lofty-ceilinged classrooms were rows of desks of the type and style familiar to pupils of the previous century. Or anyone watching a movie featuring a Victorian schoolroom.

Made for two, the wooden bench was attached with metal rods to a sloping-topped desk. There would be a level strip at the top of the scarred desk with grooves for pencils and pens and a hole for the small porcelain ink-well. Fountain pens were for the upper classes and our more prosperous teachers, and though Lazlo Biro had patented his ingenious device more than a decade before, I can't remember seeing a single one at Cottage Grove.

The school pens were also of Victorian design, and were no more than slender dowels of wood with a nib slotted on the end. It was a mark of privilege to be an ink monitor (as I was), as you got to go round all the classrooms, checking up on what was going on as well as skiving off from lessons. Another advantage was that the ink monitor was a sort of freelance armourer, providing the main ingredient for blotting paper bombs and pellets. Using a pliable wooden ruler like a miniature and simpler Roman ballista, a seasoned shootist could propel an ink pellet the full length of a classroom and replace the ruler and assume a guileless expression before the victim or teacher could turn to look for the sender. Similarly, a milk monitorship (a position I also held) was a position of privilege and real power. Like nascent bootleggers or drug dealers, monitors had control of supply and distribution and could even affect the timetable. Mates and tribute-paying children got an extra bottle or more, and a pool of milk on the top of a stove created a wondrous stink. This could delay or even cancel a lesson if the smell became unbearable and even hardy boys appeared to faint.

Where we sat was also a matter of status. From the early days at Cottage Grove I had taken possession of one of the back benches, usually sharing with my close chum Bobby Aylmer. This position had several advantages. Not only could you not be attacked from behind by ink pellets or elastic band missiles, but frequently raising the hinged lid on the desk as if to take out a book meant you could trade unobserved in cigarette cards or marbles or, when in season, conkers.

Being at the back of the class meant I could also get on with my main preoccupation, which at that time was drawing. To begin with it was always the same composition, of a knight in armour with a plumed helmet and his sword raised above his head. An arrow had just buried itself in his breastplate and there was much blood. Each day I'd start at the tip of the feather and work my way down to the arrow. I never got further because I'd give up, unsatisfied with the standard of my work. After a term or two I accepted I'd never be anything but mediocre at drawing, and gave up.

I suppose that was some sort of scene-setter of what was to come, which was a sort of Groundhog Day sequence of me starting a hobby or project or job, then becoming bored or dissatisfied and giving up. Then I'd start again, endlessly in search of something I could be really, *really* good at. I suppose you could say that the only thing I have never given up is trying to find something I am naturally very good at. The experts say that you need to do something for ten thousand hours to become really accomplished at it and they may have a point. With the exception of creative writing and trying to form a successful pop group I have never tried to be good at anything for more than ten thousand minutes, so was doomed to disappointment. It was felt more keenly when I saw real natural talent in action.

In the early 1970s when I ran the family snooker club in Southsea, I watched in wonder as Alex 'Hurricane' Higgins turned up late and drunk for an exhibition and effortlessly scored a hundred break as he magically made the white ball do his bidding. We also had a scrap before he set his car on fire, but that's another story. Because of seeing a genuine genius at work, I'd practice late into the night on the top table when the punters had gone home. I gave up after a month when my top break was a measly twenty-two and I realised I had no more than average talent for the game. This meant I could never rival or come anywhere close to the Hurricane's awesome ability, so I simply stopped trying.

Over the years I took the same approach to rugby, tennis, golf, painting, acting and becoming a rock god. If I couldn't quickly rise to be amongst the best, I didn't want to play. I left evening art classes when it was clear I had no exceptional gift. Perversely, I did show more than an average talent for boxing, but gave up immediately I lost my first bout. Curiously, the only career I have pursued doggedly for more than sixty years is creative writing. My words have been read by millions across the years, though I doubt I will ever be a blockbuster seller. Perhaps it is the search for a perfect sentence that is enough to keep the challenge and my interest alive.

~

Back in 1952, another reason for choosing a seat at the back of the class were the regular invitations to view Samantha Stott's fanny.

This was before puberty and the loss of childish innocence in matters sexual, but there was still a natural fascination for the rumours that girls varied quite dramatically from boys below the waist.

The routine was invariable, and to the best of my recall lasted for at least a term. When the coast was clear and the teacher was out of the room or absorbed with the blackboard, Samantha (again not her real name for obvious reasons) would swing round, stick her pipe-stem legs through the gap between backrest and bench seat, hoist up her skirt, pull down her knickers (they were always blue, I remember) and reveal her hairless front bottom. Bobby and I would pretend to have dropped our pens and bend down to take in and wonder at the strange sight; I remember that my predominant feeling was of pity that she had no willy to pee from or play with.

Nowadays, Bobby, I and Samantha would probably be hauled off for counselling sessions, but it was all harmless as far as intent went. It was also still some years before I was taught to masturbate by a classmate and felt the onset of an unquenchable urge which would see me trying to have sex with every desirable or just available young woman in Portsmouth. Luckily, this obsession reigned less than a decade from my first full sexual encounter until I met the love of my life and eternal soul mate.

A regrettable side effect and outcome of my awakening to the alleged joys of sex was to reject any thoughts of a rewarding or permanent career. Far more rewarding, it seemed, would be the strategy of leaving school at the earliest opportunity to get a job, buy some clobber and a motorbike and go on the pull.

But that, like my punch-up with Alex Higgins and set-to with Oliver Reed, is another Pompey Boy story which awaits the telling.

*My alma mater: Cottage Grove and the only time I held on to
the ball in my goalkeeping career*

Probably because of our relative sizes, all the teachers at Cottage Grove seemed larger than life, though some obviously were.

The head of the junior school was Mr. Hitchens. He left before I got to know him, but was said to be a very nice man. It was also said that his sudden departure was linked to a nasty rumour which had no justification. As was usual in those days, the exact nature of the rumour was never revealed.

Mr. Clarke was the music teacher, and I remember him wincing as he watched me struggling with *Bobby Shafto* on the spare (note the singular 'spare') school recorder. Upon discovering I had a totally tin ear, he consigned me to the percussion section. After a potentially serious accident with the long-handled castanets (the string broke if you clacked them too enthusiastically) I was given a tambourine as the instrument with which I could do least damage.

Miss Misslebrook (all women teachers were Misses in those days) was the English teacher. She had very fixed ideas about grammar and the use of the language. I think I gave her as much mental anguish as I did to Mr. Clarke and still can't tell if it should be 'i' before 'e' even allowing for 'c' being in the way.

The senior woman teacher was Miss Langworthy. She was an ample lady who seemed to have chosen to remain in the Edwardian era in style and manner and values. That was not unreasonable as most of our teachers would have grown up while Edward VII was on the throne.

Of all the teachers, I particularly remember Mr. Burns, who was Miss Langworthy's opposite number. It's probably a mixture of genuine recall and false memory syndrome, but across the decades I seem to see him in perfect detail. In my mind's eye he had become a character from a TV adaptation of a Dickensian novel. He would have been rather young but seemed old, and was extremely tall. He had thick, black and liberally Brylcreemed hair and wore a large, walrus moustache. His Adam's apple was as prominent as his chin was not, and with flappy wrists and other joints he was what we would have called 'gangly'. For some unaccountable reason I seem to recall small nicks and a sprinkling of razor rash on his long, chicken-like neck. Such are the vagaries of memory when you can vividly picture trifles, but whole chunks of your life are beyond recall.

I also remember Mr. Burns as having huge hands and equally outsized feet, clad in solid ankle boots in which a family of mice could comfortably have sailed across the Solent. If he had been born an animal, Mr. Burns would most certainly have been a stork or heron.

Just as clearly as the man, I remember his bicycle. It was big and black and probably older than him, and a classic sit-up-and-beg machine. A thing of wonder to me and other children because of its antiquity and intimidating size.

It was always parked in the same spot, leaning against the railings to the right of the main gates and under the shelter of a tree. Mr. Burns was a man of habit, and a small crowd of us would sometimes linger outside the gates to witness his departure ritual.

Firstly, a stack of books would be strapped on to the rear pannier, then trouser bottoms furled and cycle clips attached. Next, the pipe would be produced from the side pocket to be filled and tamped and gripped between the teeth. The bicycle would then be wheeled to the gates (it would not have done to cycle on the school premises) and a stilt-like leg swung over the saddle.

Finally, box of matches would be taken from the waistcoat pocket and the pipe lit before Mr. Burns set off to wherever he lived. He never acknowledged or reprimanded our little gang of spectators for stalking him, even if he saw us misbehaving in the streets. He was a very fair man, and knew the importance of maintaining discipline within the gates and turning a blind Nelson eye on the other side of them. I sometimes think back to those departed days and wonder what happened to him. Did he have a long and reasonably contented life, or did misfortune or tragedy strike? I hope it went well for him.

Irrational though the stance may be, I regret not knowing what happened to the many thousands who touched or passed through or lingered in my life. Just to know the headlines of their journey would be enough, for then the story would be complete and the book closed.

~

Like most teachers of that era, Mr. Burns and his male colleagues maintained order in his class by firm discipline, a system of reward and punishment and if all else failed or they were in a bad mood, physical assault. In deference to our extreme youth, physical punishment was rare, and strictly restricted to boys. It might be an almost playful cuff about the head, or a sudden rap across the knuckles with a ruler or blackboard pointer. We were rarely belittled or abused verbally, though sarcasm was often employed. Rewards included a literal pat on the head, or the granting of privileges. One was to fetch the cut-throat razor which Mr. Burns used to sharpen pencils. If you had performed particularly well you might be allowed to sharpen the razor itself. For the girls, a reward for good work might be to be allowed to leave the classroom and beat the blackboard rubber against a playground wall. The fun was to see how chalk-free the beater could get the rubber. I think modern health and safety practitioners would have something to say about the clouds of chalk dust inhaled, or indeed allowing a ten-year-old to sharpen a cut-throat razor. I don't know the accident statistics of then and now, but somehow we seemed to survive most of the perils of those careless days.

Every morning at Cottage Grove began with Assembly in the hall. Before the prayers and announcements, we would have our minds improved by listening to a piece of classical music, played on a big wind-up gramophone. If the piece was of reasonable length, it would make it through to the end, but if the handle hadn't been cranked sufficiently the tempo would slow down to a dirge. This would call for a hasty re-crank, which would usually result in a doubling of the tempo and pitch.

It was obviously an occasion of note when we were called in to an extra assembly one cold February morning. Something had happened, and we wondered if one of us had committed an offence so bad he was to be paraded and admonished before the whole school.

In fact we had been summoned to hear the grave announcement that our King was dead. We were now, Mr. Burns said, at the dawn of a new Elizabethan age.

We tried to look sad and not to cheer when the head announced the school would be closed as a mark of respect for the rest of the day.

Outside and on the way to the nearest bombsite, we discussed the prospects for next year's Coronation. We dimly realised the momentous nature of the event, but were more excited at the prospect of more days off and possibly a street party to mark the accession of our new ruler.

Credit Pete Driver, Memories of Bygone Portsmouth

An Uncommon City

For all sorts of reasons, Portsmouth is a pretty special place.

Just for a start, it's the only island city in the United Kingdom.

Also, a lot of people must like or at least have a reason for living there, as the population density is one of the highest in the UK. Portsea Island has an area of under ten square miles and a population of around 140,000. To make a basic comparison, coming up for 150 people occupy every square kilometre in Wales. In Pompey it is well over five thousand. Yep, that's five *thousand*. The nearby Isle of Wight has a smaller population but is more than fifteen times bigger.

Despite this cheek-to-jowl situation and what some visitors might allege, Pomponians can be very welcoming to outsiders, unless they diss our fair city - or hail from Southampton. But more of that traditional rivalry later.

Like all naval ports, Pompey has long played host to peoples and ships from around the world. We were multi-cultural before it was trendy, and it must have contributed significantly to the city's character and culture. Then there's a unique factor that has resulted in Portsmouth having its own accent, and even language. For centuries, young men from inland locations across Britain would be entranced by exotic tales of roving the seven seas and come to Portsmouth to join the Senior Service. They would then marry a local girl and start a family. They would also enrich the city's range of vocabulary and customs.

Perhaps because familiarity can breed contempt, local men have rarely joined the Navy, preferring to fight sailors rather than become one. There are exceptions, like my family, but it is relatively rare for anyone to be able to trace their ancestry back more than a hundred years. And this in a place which has been on the map for more than a thousand years.

Our city also has some interesting firsts and lasts, like for example:

The first-ever UFO sighting in Britain to be recognised and investigated by the Ministry of Defence occurred over Portsmouth in 1950

Sir Arthur Conan Doyle attended his first séance in Portsmouth and was converted to Spiritualism in 1887, the year the first Sherlock Holmes novel was published

Arrested in Portsmouth in 1944, Helen Duncan was the last woman in Britain to be charged with Conjuring Spirits under the 1735 Witchcraft Act

The first dry dock in England was built in Portsmouth in 1497

Tobacco was first smoked in England on Portsmouth High Street in 1604. Legend has it that a woman thought the sailors having a smoke were on fire and threw the contents of a chamber pot over them

Between 1892 and 1951, the first ship of every new class of battleship was built in Portsmouth

1953

Mount Everest is conquered by a New Zealander and his Sherpa Tenzing Norgay, but Britain takes the credit. Derek Bentley is hanged at Wandsworth Prison for his part in the 'Let him have it' murder of police constable Sidney Miles. Future Prime Minister 'Call me Tony' Blair is born. 21-year-old centre forward Tommy Taylor becomes Britain's most expensive footballer with a £29,999 transfer from Barnsley to Manchester United. Sweet rationing comes to an end.

Locally, The Cambridge pub opens in Southsea, run by the local legendary-landlord-to-be, Johnny Duthwaite. Gosport trumpeter Nat Gonella and his Georgians are appearing at South Parade Pier. Over the road at the Savoy, George Turner (another local legend in the making) celebrates five years as manager. Popular recordings of the year include 'Your Cheatin' Heart' by Hank Williams, 'That's Amore' by Dean Martin and 'Don't let the Stars Get in Your Eyes' by Perry Como.

George V's widow and consort Queen Mary dies, and the nation celebrates the Coronation of Queen Elizabeth II.

I am assured that the year of 1953 was of the usual duration. In my memory, it seemed to go on and on. Perhaps that's because it encapsulated so many of the golden memories of childhood before adolescence let reality into our lives.

It would also be true to say a lot happened in that twelve months, and the year was made especially memorable by the formal enthronement of our new Queen. Perhaps more importantly for children, 1953 was also made very special by the end of sweet rationing and the host of neighbourhood knees-ups marking the Coronation.

We had acquired a taste for street parties and public demonstrations of joy in the previous decade with VE Day (Victory in Europe) and VJ Day (Victory in Japan). Now it was time to make merry again, and the nation was more than ready for it. In the grey days when some wartime rationing was still in place, it was a good excuse for a little over-indulgence.

With the promise of jelly and trifle and cakes and sugar-laden fizzy drinks, we children were agog with excitement, and the street parties were almost as eagerly anticipated as Christmas. It also seemed the adults were getting just as worked-up with the opportunity to show their love and loyalty of the new Queen - and the monarchy in general. Almost every house on my way to Cottage Grove made some form of declaration, with front widows awash with paper Union Flags and golden crowns and photographs and drawings of Elizabeth and Prince Philip.

Perhaps it was because we had got through a war it looked for a long time we would lose that there was an overarching sense of national unity and self-pride. For whatever reason, the Coronation was a perfect way of demonstrating our love and loyalty. The Royal Family had represented everything we were fighting for in our stand against tyranny, and there was a tangible feeling of admiration and love for the young woman who would lead us into the uncertain future. I can't recall hearing a single Republican sentiment at the prospect, but then nobody would have risked voicing one in public. Thanks to William Brown books and the popular comics, our only idea of a Republican or anti-monarchist was a 'Bolshie' (Bolshevik*), always shown as a shifty-looking, swarthy man in a black cape and steepled hat, holding a fizzing bomb.

As the big day approached we practiced waving our miniature Union Jacks and lined up at school to be presented with a Coronation mug (I still have mine) and a slim blue book telling us all about our new Queen. Commonwealth postage stamps bearing Her Majesty's head soared in swap-value, and sometimes even smutty jokes were common. The most repeated (if not always understood) in our playground went like this:

Teller: 'Did you know Prince Phillip has an eight-inch willy?'

All present: 'God Save The Queen!'

I don't think it would be possible for a child of today to imagine what excitement the prospect of an open-air feast of jelly, blancmange, sherbet lemonade and cake and fish paste sandwiches generated. Money was tight in every working-class family, and availability of sweet treats even tighter. Eight long years on from the end of the war, sugar had yet to be de-rationed. It had been tried in 1949, but demand so far exceeded supplies that rationing was reinstated after just four months. For this very special event, the government had made a one-off allocation of extra sugar to make more confectionery.

Predictably, sales of sweets that year increased by

One hundred million pounds (more than £2 billion at today's prices).

Bolsheviks were originally active supporters of the Russian Revolution in 1917, but the description became applied to any anti-monarchist or anarchist groups or individuals. So much were they hated by pro-monarchists that the word 'Bolshie' became an adjective for any generally objectionable attitude or behaviour.

~

Although residents had dressed their streets for significant dates and occasions since Queen Victoria's Golden Jubilee in 1887, the idea of street parties became increasingly popular after the 'Peace Teas' of 1919. The nation having got the taste for open-air beanos, they came thick and fast from the 1935 Silver Jubilee of George V, followed just two years later by the Coronation of George VI. Then came VE and VJ Days, the Festival of Britain in 1951 and now the Coronation of Elizabeth II.

Not all streets held a party and the nearest to my home would be in Belmont Street, which lay on my walk to school. I can't remember how children were allocated a place, but by craftily adopting an alias I managed to find a seat at two parties. The weather was good and the celebration was everything we could have hoped for. Everyone played their part, and I can't remember a single blow or even a reprimand from any of the parents. An upright piano had been manhandled into the street, and there was a spoons player and an old man with a violin who was said to have once played for a proper orchestra. There was also a barrel of beer on stocks, tapped and ready.

As dusk fell the lanterns were lit and the singalong began. Those with a party piece performed it; and others became more emboldened as the ale, shandy and ginger beer flowed. It was a day and night to be remembered.

Almost exactly fifty years later I did a tour of Portsmouth street parties to make a documentary programme for the local television station. Just as half a century earlier, the parents and helpers had put a huge effort into making the day a special one, and you could see the children were enthralled if sometimes a little bemused. The food was far more exotic, the music from state-of-the-art music systems with huge sets of loudspeakers and the adults drank prosecco and lager. But the spirit was the same, and showed that in some things, Britain hadn't changed all that much.

What's in a Name?

The origin of the official name of our home city should be obvious. Portsmouth is a port at the mouth of an inlet at a place called 'Port Sea'. Printable names for we citizens include 'Portsmouthians', 'Pomponians' and even 'Pompeyites'. The denizens of Southampton have a selection of much more exotic names for us.

For this memoir I have mainly employed 'Portmuthians'. This is mainly because *The Portmuthian* has been the name of our oldest and poshest grammar school's house magazine since 1883, and they should know.

Much more divisive and mysterious are the origins of the nickname 'Pompey' for the city and soccer team. Some of the claims seem unlikely, some almost farcical.

One in the far-fetched category is that a group of Portsmouth-based seamen climbed a pillar in Egypt around 1781. The pillar was (erroneously) named 'Pompey's Pillar' after the great Roman General, and the climbers were dubbed 'The Pompey Boys'. The name, so the story goes, was later applied to the town from where the climbers came. Against this explanation is that the column was very smooth and would have been near-impossible to climb even by an 18th-century Jack Tar topman.

Another contender concerns the wedding of Catherine of Braganza to Charles II at Portsmouth Cathedral in 1662. A member of the Portuguese Royal Family, part of Catherine's dowry was the port of Bombay, and it is said that sailors in her party observed the similarity between the two ports. They dubbed the town 'Bom Bhia', which became anglicised into 'Pompey.' Hmmm, really?

More credible explanations involving naval custom and practice and drunken pronunciations include:

~ All RN ships arriving at the port were required to make an entry in the log. The exact location would be registered as 'Portsmouth Point'. Over the years the entry was abbreviated to 'Pom. P.'

~ *La Pompee* was a French ship captured in 1793 and used as a prison hulk.

~ Another French connection in that volunteer firemen used to practice on Southsea Common in the late 18th century. French for 'fireman' is *pompier*, and as France had the first modern Fire Services, it is possible that the British firefighters adopted the name in the early days.

~ 'Pompey' is no more than a seaman's drunken, slurred mis-pronunciation of 'Portsmouth Point'.

Of all the above, I prefer the 'Pom. P' explanation, as it ticks all the boxes for how nicknames emerge and become established.

~

We can't leave the subject without mention of perhaps the most unlikely if somehow pleasing explanation for the town and soccer team's nickname. It is probably pleasing to me because it has particularly nostalgic connections:

From the age of eight, part of my religious observances were regular attendances at various churches, missions and halls. It wasn't that my parents were particularly devout or wanted me to be. It meant they could get me off their hands for a couple of hours on a weekday evening or Sunday afternoon. It might seem strange to modern readers that I was allowed to wander around the city after dark and on my own at that relatively tender age, but times and people were different then.

Twice a week there would be cub scout meetings at St Jude's hall in Marmion Road, when we would be expected to turn up with piles of newspapers scavenged from around the locality. Old Skip the scoutmaster looked not unlike W. C. Fields in shorts and a dodgy woggle. In my mind's eye he also had the biggest and most pitted strawberry-like drinker's nose I had seen then or since. With stained sweater and pipe-stem knobbly knees exposed, he would sit on a stool with a weighing balance in one hand, waiting to accept our offerings.

I can't remember which charity or good cause was supposed to benefit from the weekly collection, but I suspect at least some of it went towards his drinking fund.

There were also more serious rumours about Old Skip, but when I approached he always seemed more interested in the size of my bundle of newspapers than me.

~

At more spiritually-centred locations, the entry price would be a stern lecture on the perils of straying from the straight and narrow. The reward would be a tract, a cup of tea and sometimes even an iced bun.

I don't know if they are still common currency at Sunday school meetings (if indeed they still happen) but tracts were little illustrated cards with a religious theme. They would show bands of angels and cherubs doing good works or a saint's gruesome martyrdom, and always a suitable homily such as 'Pray Most For Those Who Hurt You.'

In an age before magical devices with names like X-Box, Playstation and Googlefart to pass the time, tracts were collected as avidly as stamps and cigarette ('fag') cards. Fag cards bore illustrations and details of famous soccer and cricket players, racing drivers and jockeys.

Some were cartoons, and for a while I thought all famous sportsmen had huge heads and tiny bodies. As the name implies, the cards came in cigarette packets and in seemingly unlimited variety and number. This meant we spent a good deal of time in the playground or back of the classroom doing deals and swapping cards for ones we needed, or for sweets or sometimes for a temporary cessation of bullying. Understandably, we spent a lot of time encouraging our parents to smoke more by helpfully bringing their packet to where they sat, or stealing individual cigarettes.

A favourite local venue for tract-collecting was Miss Earn's classes in the Bethesda Mission tin-roofed hut in one of the side streets off Castle Road. I remember her as a little, round, rubicund and very kindly if terminally earnest woman. In my memory she wore John Lennon-style round glasses and a bonnet and shawl-cape in the style of the then Salvation Army uniform.

But even more rewarding than a visit to Miss Earn's was the Sunday afternoon tract-collecting trip to Aggie Weston's.

Dame Agnes Weston had been a leading light in The National Temperance League, with a particular interest in keeping sailors and alcohol apart. Her life's mission was doomed, but she did provide a popular refuge for matelots on shore leave when in 1881, she opened a Sailor's Rest in Portsmouth.

Seventy years on and Aggie Weston's was still doing good works, and a popular Sunday afternoon venue for me and other kids on the make. There and in return for a stern talking-to with a selection of bored or drunk sailors, I and my chums would get a cup of tea, a tract and an iced bun.*

Another attraction was that our route took us from the Town Station into the Guildhall Square, where we would make straight for Verrecchia's for a threepenny cornet of the best ice cream in the world. But more of that legendary institution later.

Back to the source of our city's nickname, and the story goes that a huddle of hungover sailors were being given a lecture on the Roman General, Pompey the Great. When the talk reached his assassination in 48 BC, a still-tipsy seaman shouted out 'Poor old Pompey'. This raised a laugh, and according to some sources, is the origin of the name by which our city is known wherever in the world British sailors go on a runashore**.

It may be a load of nonsense, but it is, I think, an interesting option.

There were any number of what were generally called 'fancies' at the time, but the iced bun seemed ubiquitous as a sweet treat. Always taken, of course, with a nice cup of tea and two sugars.

Historical fact: In those days, drinking tea without sugar was a very suspicious activity and close to a criminal offence.

**'Runashore' was originally sailor-talk for any visit to a port when in dock. Over the years, it came to mean an event involving calling in on lots of pubs and drinking shedloads of beer.*

Very swappable: fag card stars with normal-size heads

A fresh spring morning, and a small boy dawdles to school. He's preoccupied with sorting his collection of cigarette cards and planning how to get the best swap for a duplicate of England wicket-keeper Godfrey Evans.

The boy has a basin cut* and wears a much-washed khaki shirt and baggy shorts held up with a snake belt.** On his feet are a pair of very scuffed white plimsols (the pre-runners of trainers). They offered little protection when exploring a bomb-dump, but were very light and when wearing them you felt you could fly. Although fairly clean when I left home, my knees are already scratched and filthy from stopping off to explore the crypt of the bombed-out church near the junction.

I know parents who take their kids to and from school by car when it's in the next road. In my childhood, all working-class families were car-less and lucky to have a bike between them. Believe it or not, reader of today, but at nine I was considered old enough to make the four-times-a-day journey even though it included what was then considered a busy road.

Nowadays, the stretch where Elm Grove and King's Road meet is a place of mostly shabby shops and bland, boxy blocks of flats thrown up soon after World War II. Inevitably, it's also a racetrack of lorries and cars and buses, slowed only by accidents or frequent traffic jams.

In 1953, a blind man could have crossed Elm Grove in safety as long as he waved his white stick fairly vigorously. For me at nine, it was a relaxed solo journey, punctuated by stoppings-off at any of our local adventure playgrounds. Then, they were known as bomb damages, bombsites or bomb-dumps.

Long before the attentions of the Luftwaffe and in the high Victorian era, this part of Southsea was a lofty and elegant thoroughfare boasting any number of fine residential and commercial premises. There was an imposing church and a grand and respectable 'gin palace' public house and, near to the junction with Castle Road, Arthur Conan Doyle practiced as a doctor at Number One, Bush Villas. There he would consult with patients in between sessions of writing the first Sherlock Holmes novel, *A Study in Scarlet.* He also found time to cycle with the local Velo club, enjoy games of cricket and bowls, and he even played in goal for the team which was to become Portsmouth Football Club.

At around the same time and in a remarkable coincidence, another celebrated Victorian literary figure worked briefly in a nearby haberdashery store. H. G. Wells hated every moment at Hyde's Emporium, but his experiences inspired him to write *The Wheels of Chance*, *The History of Mr Polly* and *Kipps*.

Another celebrated local figure and hero of the Battle of Trafalgar (according to my mother) was our ancestor Tom Pitt the Elder. I know it to be true that as a young man he had walked over Portsdown Hill to join Nelson's Navy at the turn of the century and taken lodgings in Bush Villas. I also know from contemporary records that Old Tom was a ship's tailor, which meant that when not sewing bodies in canvas shrouds he would repair officer's clothes. According to Mum, he was personally responsible for the Admiral Lord Nelson cutting such a dashing figure.

As can be seen by the photograph of me on Southsea seafront in my woollen bathers, all pre-adolescent boys in those days wore their hair in what was called a basin-cut style. Later it would be known as a short-back-and sides, but still looked as if a pudding basin had been put on the victim's head and any trace of hair below the rim sheared and hacked off. This had actually happened in the previous century, and must have been a torment for boys like me with over-sized heads. In our more progressive times, boys' hair was cut by mum or dad without the basin but with the same result. The torturer-in-chief would use kitchen scissors and the family comb, or even special implements with serrated edges and exotic names made for the purpose. The manufacturers made exaggerated claims for their performance, but the results were just as painful in physical and visual terms. The outcome made a thin boy look like a human mop, or a fat one like Kenneth Branagh in the title role of Henry V.

**All through the Fifties, a snake belt was almost compulsory wear for all small boys.

First appearing in the Great War, the clasp was 'S' shaped and fitted into a hook on the belt. Its main advantage was that it could be released quickly in an emergency. By the time I and every other boy in the school and country were wearing them, the s-shape buckle had become a stylised snake. The belt itself would be divided into two horizontal coloured stripes, and actor Michael Bates famously used one to keep his turban in place in the very un-politically correct TV comedy series, It Ain't Half Hot, Mum.

~

Parents who could afford it took their male children to a proper barber's shop. I don't remember what happened to girls, but my wife tells me that most mothers didn't cut their daughter's hair. That happened at the ladies' hairdresser. I do remember that the standard style was, like Sheila Parker's, a side parting, cut below the ears and held in place with a slide or grip.

For boys, one or more parents would escort their son to the premises to make sure they got their money's worth, and that their boy didn't abscond on route and spend the money on sweets. Sometimes a crafty child who was allowed to go for a haircut alone would get a friend to do it and split the money. This was a risky business especially if the operator had no access to proper tools. The ever-enterprising Jack Tinker set up shop in his garden shed, using grass clippers. Oddly, the results looked no worse than those achieved with the Clip-o-Matic de Luxe ('Results Just Like a Costly Visit to the Barber's!').

Unusually I looked forward to my visits to Mr Floyd's tonsorial establishment, which occupied the front room of a terraced house in Great Southsea Street. My enthusiasm for the visit perhaps because it gave me my first access to an exclusively male world.

In what had been the front parlour, the atmosphere would be dense with pipe and tobacco smoke, and the odour just as thick. In the way that all Indian restaurants and ashtrays smell the same, so did all barbers shops, and I can shut my eyes and immediately recall the distinctive twang. It was always the same mix of stale and fresh tobacco, singed hair, unwashed male bodies and farts, Brylcreem and the teeth-meltingly sharp aroma of the atomised pomade delivered from a bulb-operated spray as a dramatic climax to the operation. Then and as Mr Floyd whipped off the sheet with a flourish and got rid of any stray hairs with a brush kept in the top pocket of his smock, he would offer to provide any additional goods or services. It was some years before I realised that 'Something for the weekend, sir?' was code for the availability of contraceptives.

Also on offer would be the chance to have a punt on a dog or horse. Off-course betting being illegal, bookies' runners would visit places where men gathered to take bets or pay out winnings, and a barber's shop was a perfect location. Along with his fee, Mr Floyd would take the stake and folded slips of paper naming the meeting time and chosen runner. When I was a little older, I would be trusted to take my dad's nap selection to Mr Floyd's. I bet a child of today could have no idea of what it was like to be sneaking along the route, feeling that mix of fear and excitement while alert to the dangers of apprehension by gangs of undercover and plain-clothes police officers with nothing better to do than lie in wait for child bookies' runners.

War Games: Me and neighbour Melvin Townsend.
Note the pre-snake belt braces

Funny Money

For those born after 'D' for Decimalisation Day in 1971, a word about the wonderfully whacky world of Pounds, Shillings and Pence. Or as we said then and just to make it an even more confusing, LSD.

To us, Britain's long-established currency seemed straightforward and even logical, but in hindsight the old system was more than a little archaic and certainly confusing to foreign visitors. I think a lot of people counted that as a plus. It's sometimes nice to be different and do things your own way, which is of course just one of the reasons why we chose to leave the EU.

~

Starting at the bottom, the smallest pre-decimal coin in both size and value was the farthing. Don't ask me where the name came from. Even in 1953 it wasn't worth a lot, but from a child's perspective it would still buy a single blackjack chew or a small liquorice stick.

Two farthings made a half-penny, and, quite logically, two ha'pennies made a penny piece. These coins were known as 'coppers' because of their colour and content, or 'clods' because of their weight.

Are you still with me? Good.

Three pennies made the value of a strange little yellow-ish coin called unsurprisingly, a threepenny bit. For some reason, 'thrupenny bits' became slang for a part of the female anatomy, as in 'Blimey, look at the size of them thrupenny bits!'

Next came the silver coins, or more accurately, silver in appearance. The sixpenny piece or 'tanner' was small and worth, as you might suspect, six pennies. Twelve pennies made a shilling or (for some unknown reason) a 'bob' and two shillings made a florin, or two-bob-bit.

Next in value came the half-crown piece, which was worth two shillings and sixpence. Just to make things more complicated, there was no longer a crown to justify the name of the half-crown, although we commonly referred to five bob as an 'Oxford Scholar'. This was rhyming slang for a dollar, and the term was used because for a long time you could get four USA dollars to the Pound Stirling.

Next came the ten shilling and one-pound notes. A five-pound note or fiver would regularly appear in wage packets, but although it had been in circulation since 1759, a ten-pound note was a real rarity. Given the average wage in 1953 was £9, finding a note of that denomination in our pay packet would be like paying today's average earner with a single £500 note.

Finally, there was the Guinea*, which - like the Crown - no longer actually existed. It had been withdrawn from circulation in 1877 but was retained as an honorary term or 'money of account'. It represented a sum of one pound and one shilling, and was a staple in posh environments like horse racing circles and auction rooms. A number of the professional classes still charged and got paid nominally in guineas, and my wife's first weekly wage at the solicitor's office in which she worked in 1965 was one guinea.

In case you wondered, the coin got its name because it was made mostly from gold mined in the Guinea area of West Africa.

Pricing the Past

Just one of the drawbacks of getting older is that everything seems so expensive. Of course it is when compared with half a century or so ago, but we oldies tend to forget that incomes and pensions have generally gone up in proportion.

However, a major head-banger is the change in relative values of some things, even allowing for inflation. For a very good instance, in 1970 we paid £10,750 for a vast, five-bedroom house in Southsea. Nowadays it would set you back around £450,000. Astonishing, eh? But you have to remember that my wage was £20 a week, so the purchase price represented 10 years of my gross income, which was also the total amount coming into the home. Nowadays, some households have two or more wage-earners to pay the bills...or are not troubled by taking on huge loans. When we were married, most women stayed at home to look after the house and children, and being in debt was frowned upon. Any income they did bring in would not be taken into consideration when assessing the allowable mortgage amount.

Just to complicate things further, houses have gone up in (perceived) value out of all proportion to inflation. That's what makes it all so complicated when looking at the cost of living and what life was like in days gone-by. What made our values and views so different then was that, while some things were a lot cheaper (like house prices) a lot of things like clothing and shoes cost a great deal more than nowadays. Then you have to factor in that we had far less expectations - or opportunities to splash out. No family I knew would even think of going to foreign parts on holiday, or much further from home than a B&B in distant Blackpool. More likely they would take a chalet or caravan on Hayling Island or even go 'abroad' to the Isle of Wight.

So, if you want to try to understand about the past and relative values, you have to remember that attitudes and expectations were a lot different in the distant past...and the relative cost of things helped shape our society. If you don't get that, you can't begin to really understand what life was like then.

If nothing else, the list below gives an indication of what some everyday things cost in the 1950s, and I've added present-day equivalent of those amounts (i.e. allowing for inflation) so you can see how much some values (like housing) have changed. Another complication is that, as you can see, the inflation-adjusted average wage for 1953 was just £11,000 at today's prices. In fact the average wage nowadays is more than double that. And, unlike in 1953, it is common for both husband and wife or partners in any house to work, vastly increasing the buying power coming through the door in comparison with those far-off days.

Sincere thanks for the personal recollection of everyday prices in 1953 are due to members of the Memories of Bygone Portsmouth forum

Disclaimer: *Remember that most of the prices are typical rather than average prices, and would have varied across the nation and depending on the size or quality. You also have to appreciate that the figures in the right-hand column are approximately what those things would cost at today's prices* **if they had retained the same value.** *To say in terms of resentful envy that your great-great-grandfather bought a house for 3/6d in 1923 is not the point. We can only work in rough* averages here but must factor in relative values then and now. A typical example of how things change because of technology is that buying a tiny black and white TV in 1953 would set you back around £1500 at today's values. Of course, you can get a glorious, de-luxe all singing-and-dancing cinema-screen sized set for a quarter that amount nowadays.

As you will also see, in 1953 an unremarkable bicycle cost over six hundred pounds at today's prices. So, in summary, house prices have soared in real terms since 1953, while tellies, shoes and bicycles can be had for a mere fraction of the relative price they once commanded. I might seem to be overstressing the point, but the relative costs of things to a family on an average wage is key to understanding life in the 1950s in Portsmouth - and everywhere else in Britain. Like, for instance, why people re-soled their shoes in those days rather than chuck them away and buy a new pair when they grew tired of them. And why TV ownership was so low.

A final, final reminder. The prices in the left-hand column are what some things cost (very approximately) in 1953, in 'new pence' for the sake of younger readers. The right-hand column shows what those 1953 figures would be nowadays *had their relative values stayed the same.* I've taken this approach as it gives a dramatic indication of how some things have rocketed in relative value, while others seem far cheaper.

Average wage	£450	£11,620p
Average House	£1,800	£49,000p
New car (Ford Popular)	£391	£17,000p
Bicycle (Raleigh Trent Tourist)	£24	£619.73p
Gallon of petrol (five litres)	22p	£5.75p
Pint of beer	5p	£1.29p
Pint of milk	3p	75p
Large loaf of bread	3p	75p
2lb bag of sugar	3p	75p

Cheese (a pound)	5p	£1.29p
6lb potatoes	5p	£1.29p
Pound of butter	18p	£5.16p
Walls Family Block ice cream	7p	£1.72p
Eggs (12)	22p	£5.75p
Man's haircut	5p	54p
Ladies' home perm	37p	£9.25p
Man's shoes (brogues)	£3.00p	£77.47p
Lady's shoes (Clark's court heel)	£3. 25p	£83.92p
Television	£60.00p	£1550.00p
Packet of cigarettes (10)	7p	£1.72p
Postage stamp	1p	27p

If they could have seen what the future would bring, the price of a house in Castle Road (or anywhere else) nowadays would be beyond belief to the people who lived in them in the 1950s.

Mind you, we oldies also tend to think in terms of what cost what in earlier years. The other day I saw the asking price for a modest dwelling near our old home and nearly fell off my chair.

Another irritation of surviving to a ripe old age is the realisation of how rich you would be if you had done things differently and collected and kept the right things. Especially those things made of bricks and mortar. These days Castle Road is classy and in estate agent parlance, my old home is set in a very desirable conservation area of Regency residences. In the early 1950s, our road was not so valued. It was in much need of restoration and comprised a handful of bomb sites and a mix of rented and owned properties. The state of repair of the houses varied greatly, as did the families who occupied them. Some properties that were considered suitable for occupation then would be condemned as slums nowadays. Some were in such a state they looked as if they had suffered severe structural damage in a bombing raid.

Many of the houses in Castle Road which survived the attention of the Luftwaffe were centuries old, and an interesting melange of architectural styles. Probably because of their size, a lot of them were home to large families or used as an extra form of income. Some had the front room kitted out as an informal shop; others took in sewing work or washing or children. One of the houses near where we lived seemed to have a constant flow of male visitors, particularly sailors. When I asked an older boy why the lady who lived there was so popular, he laughed and said she was a prozzy and it was a red-light house. At eight, I didn't know what a prozzy was, so supposed she might be a professional photographer, taking and developing portraits for all those sailors to send home to their mums and girlfriends.

Given the lack of TV reality shows and mobile phones, climbing over walls and sneaking a look through people's front windows was a popular pastime for children, and Castle Road offered many interesting peep shows. The curtains on the red-light lady's front windows were always tightly drawn, but others allowed investigation and speculation based on what was going on in the front room. A good example was that I and my gang suspected a Bolshevik was at work in the basement of the large house next to a corner bomb-dump. According to the placard beside the front door, the occupant was a watch and clock repairer, but we suspected that was a front. We would sneak down the steps and watch him, tiny screwdriver in hand as he bent over a collection of mechanical parts spread out on a bench. He might claim to be putting the innards of an old clock right; we reckoned it could be the timing mechanism for a bomb, perhaps destined to be planted on a ship in the dockyard. In fact, if not an anarchist he could be a Red spy, sent from the Kremlin to wreak havoc at the nation's premier naval base.

Further along and past the red-light lady's house and where a bicycle repairer plied his trade in his mother's parlour was what was claimed to be a grocery supplies depot. There was no sign above the double doors, through which would be a constant flow of goods to be loaded into a procession of anonymous and ancient delivery vans. The suspicious thing was that the vans were always loaded after dark. Despite staking the place out while pretending to play marbles in the opposite gutter, we never found evidence the place had a more sinister purpose than delivering to shops after closing time. But to us, it was more likely a distribution point for illegally brewed beer and moonshine whisky. The fact that Prohibition in America had been repealed twenty years before and never applied in Britain did nothing to put us off using our imaginations to make things more exciting than they were in what was still a fairly monochrome world. But there was one fascinating home enterprise in the road which didn't need enhancing.

In a decrepit old property just before the corner pub there lived a pair of commercial artists. At least once a day we would sneak into the forecourt and up on to the window ledge and sneak a look into the front room. Sometimes the couple would be painting slavering lions attacking and being shot at point blank range by brave white hunters in long khaki shorts and pith helmets. Or it would be a giant space rocket, alien monster or World War II tank, its barrel belching fire and fury. In those pre-TV and commercial radio days, the couple's business was to create posters and advertisements for films coming to Portsmouth. By far their most impressive creations were the larger-than-life, cut-out illustrations of the stars of coming attractions. I particularly remember a giant Roy Rogers astride a rearing Trigger, and a drooling green monster which was the star of *The Beast from 20,000 fathoms*.

The lower panes of the bay window were permanently whitewashed in the way people would maintain privacy when re-decorating, and I and my chums would stand on the sill gazing in wonder as the illustrations came to life. I think it may have been this early exposure to creative endeavour that helped form my ambition to be a world-famous and very rich painter. In later years when I told my career master, he sniffed and said he had never heard of any of his pupils getting rich by painting houses.

Although often chased away, we were very proud of our neighbours, perhaps because their work forged a sort of connection between us and the heroes of the films they promoted. When passing the Gaumont or Troxy cinemas, we would be sure to tell anyone who would listen that the placards *for Abbot and Costello Go to Mars* or *The Titfield Thunderbolt* had been made by our artistic neighbours.

~

The family home at 26, Castle Road was a substantial terraced property, laid out over three floors. Family, friends and lodgers were always coming and going, and it is a comment on the times that the key dangled conveniently from a piece of string hanging on the back of the front door. All you had to do was reach through the letterbox to let yourself in. This was common practice, either because people were more trusting then, or perhaps put off by the cost of having duplicate keys cut. Or maybe they didn't think they had anything worth stealing, but for whatever reason, that's how it was.

It is, though, a myth that we were all honest as the days were long then or that there was no looting during the Blitz. I particularly remember a coat disappearing from the hook in the passageway by the front door. When my mother ascertained I hadn't donated it to the O'Kelly family (*see later*) she was incandescent with rage. She wrote a blistering letter to the Portsmouth News, and even cycled to their headquarters in Stanhope Road to deliver it and get an assurance from the editor that it would be printed in a prominent position. But in spite of her wrath, the key on the string stayed where it was.

~

I liked it that number 26 was always a hive of activity, with my mother a very busy queen bee.

As well as the housework and looking after us, waitressing at outside catering events and giving piano and dancing lessons, she ran our home as a quirky lodging house-cum-B&B and even sometimes hostel. In those less pretentious days, people who paid to stay with you for more than a holiday were called 'lodgers', not 'guests'. Travelling fairground and circus folk would regularly arrive, providing they met Mother's criteria. 'Proper' circus acts were admitted but not those who put the Big Top up and down. Travelling fairground people who ran their own sideshows were usually welcome, unless their attraction was, in her opinion, vulgar or 'common'. Like most people in those days, Mother had fixed ideas on who should mix with whom. Naval officers were always welcome, and even ratings provided they were respectably married and paid on the dot.

My mother was anything but greedy, but without the various safety nets and credit facilities of today, most ordinary families lived in fear of running out of money. And there was the social stigma of not being able to pay the bills.

When lodgers were particularly scarce and my dad out of work, Mother would take on yet another job. I remember her using the front room for music, singing and dancing lessons although she had no training in either activity. Once I remember her becoming an importer of hand-operated food slicers and targeting guest houses along Southsea seafront.

Times were tight and working-class families could or would not pay for top quality accommodation, so the owners of all those Homeleas and Bideawhiles and Sea Breezes had to practice real economies. It was the norm for the proprietor to mix butter with margarine to make it go further, and the appeal of a food slicer which would deliver almost transparent slices of cheese and meat and tomatoes was clear. The board and hand-cranked saw-toothed wheel were made in Sweden and my mother naturally blonde, so as a sales aid she would pretend to be from that country. She couldn't speak a word of Swedish, but, as she pointed out, nor would any of her potential customers, and she was good at accents.

Class Acts

A lot of people seem to think modern Britain is a very class-conscious place. They should have been around in the middle of the last century.

Nowadays, we are categorised more by wealth and fame than by what we do for a living. Neither are we judged by what school we went to and how good an education we were given there. Indeed, inverse snobbery dictates the opposite, and fame and wealth are the criteria. A TV reality 'star' (i.e. someone lacking in any discernible talent except for being unembarrassable) may earn ten times the income of an MP or head teacher while thinking that Scotland is the capital of Wales. Also, some tradesmen value their services at a price beyond rubies. Recently I went on the waiting list for the services of a plumber who charges £200 a day for his specialist attention (breaks and travelling time included).

You may think that the breakdown of the class system and the different ways we judge people are a good or bad thing, but in 1953, class-ism was still going strong. Writing in 1937 in *The Road to Wigan Pier*, George Orwell claimed to be Lower Upper Middle Class. In my childhood, the classifications had thinned out, but not that much.

At the very bottom of the pile were the Unemployed Poor, while at the top were the Unemployed Rich. In between were a series of social divisions, each with its own sub-divisions. Income was often an indicator of level, but not always.

Next up from the unemployed poor (vagrants, tramps, beggars and permanent invalids) was the great mass known as the Working Class. At the bottom of this class came those who worked as general labourers ('navvies') or in other allegedly unskilled occupations. Next came craftsmen and other people who worked with their hands but had a set of skills. Roughly at their level would be people who managed workers in occupations where people got their hands dirty. This would include foremen in factories or on building sites.

Next came the Lower-Middle Classes. This was the most class-ist group of all and would mainly consist of what were known as White Collar Workers. This section of society considered themselves way above any member of the working classes, whatever they did or how skilled they were. To prove it, they wore a suit and tie to work and never got their hands dirty. The group included clerks and salesmen and shop assistants. As before, there were several categories within this group. Your status or level of self-regard would depend on factors like how posh was the shop in which you served, what sort of goods you dealt in ... and even how much contact you had with the customers. Floor walkers would look down their noses at managers of individual departments, and they would look down their noses at their staff. Floating somewhere in between working-class and lower middle-class status would be farmers, policemen and shopkeepers.

Then there were the Middle-Middle-Classes, a much easier group to define and categorise. The mainstay were teachers and more elevated white-collar workers like office managers. Slightly above them but in the same category would come solicitors and bank managers.

Whichever rung on the status ladder they occupied, all classes would look up with sometimes sick-making cap-doffing deference to members of the Upper Middle Class. This grouping would include surgeons, barristers, landed gentry and the Idle Rich.

Then there was the rarified atmosphere occupied by

the Aristocracy. They usually had few skills or attainments other than being born to the owners of ancient titles and grand but often decrepit stately homes. Even then they were a threatened species, faced with a future of turning their homes into theme parks and admitting the great unwashed to gawp at how grandly their ancestors lived.

Right at the top of this class pyramid were, of course, the Monarchy, although there were some aristocrats with a long history in the country who actually considered themselves to be superior to the Johnny-come-lately Windsors. But to most people, our Royal family were beyond criticism. We understood and appreciated that their job was to act as a symbol of all that was great about our nation and its history and heritage. Regardless of changing times and the antics of some dodgy members of the Royal Family, they were and still are the glue that helps hold our nation together. Nearly all my life I have watched with admiration and even devotion the woman who has given her life to duty. Those who decry our monarchical system should ask themselves why our system is so admired by people of so many Republics around the world.

The City of Pubs

Once upon a time, Portsmouth was known throughout the world for its public houses. Many sailors from foreign parts saw no more of the city than the insides of the pubs nearest to the Dockyard gates.

In those far-off days, Pompey was said to have more public houses than lamp posts. It is certainly a fact that at one time there were a thousand taverns, inns, hostelries and plain boozers trading in our small island, and they all made a living. Changing times and tastes, a shrinking Royal Navy and even the Luftwaffe all helped deplete the city's licensed estate, but we still have more than our fair share of pubs.

In years to come, I'd help make, deliver, serve and drink oceans of beer, cider and stout and run my own bars, clubs and pubs. In the early Fifties I'd often be found on a pub threshold with a packet of Smith's Crisps and a bottle of fizzy lemonade. My dad liked being in pubs, but in those days children were not allowed on the premises. On special occasions like birthdays and anniversaries, they might take their wives into the Lounge. Rightly or wrongly, the pub, and especially the public bar, was a place for men to escape the demands of family, home and work.

For hundreds of years, public houses have provided a rich source of information about the development of society; in the 1950s, the attitudes and divisions within the classes were reflected in the layout and facilities of nearly all Portsmouth's public houses.

Nowadays and no matter how much the décor recalls

nostalgic images of the past, all customers invariably rub shoulders in one large bar. In my childhood, even the smallest corner boozers would segregate their clients. A hundred years ago there would be up to five separate bars to keep the classes apart. In my day it had mostly gone down to two, but the demarcations were rigidly clear.

The public bar would be the preserve of people who worked with their hands, and in some Pompey pubs that would include pickpockets and burglars. The Public was invariably a male-only preserve, unless the landlord was okay with admitting working girls. This would usually be in the town centre where drunken sailors like to spend their money like, erm, drunken sailors.

In the typical public bar there would be a dartboard and perhaps a bar billiards table and shove ha'penny board. The floor would be covered with linoleum, ('lino') pockmarked by a million cigarettes, and the nicotine-stained ceiling would give an idea of what the insides of the customers' lungs must look like. On tap would be watery beer and thin, acidic bitter, while the back shelves would offer mainly half-pint bottles of brown and light ales. Pints of draught beer would be served in sleeved glasses (i.e. no handles). On the counter, popular snacks like pickled onions and eggs and world-weary pies would be on display. A running gag was that the pies were kept in glass cabinets to stop them escaping. To add to the atmosphere and the colour of the ceiling and damage to table tops and floor, smoking was almost compulsory.

On the other side of a thin partition would be the Lounge, and a different world. It was all flock wallpaper and dimpled pint and half pint glasses with the luxury of a handle. There would be carpets on the floor and pictures on the wall, and the Gents and Ladies would often have soap and towels and toilet paper to hand. The barmen would be kitted out with shirts that had collars, and even ties. In particular, the barmaids would dress more discreetly than on the other side of the dividing wall. To reflect the higher quality of the surroundings and also to make the clientele feel superior, there would be a penny or two surcharge on all drinks. Many people were happy to pay the extra just to show they could afford to. When I was of drinking age I and my mates were always keen to buck the system and would often buy our pints in the public and take them next door. It wasn't because we liked the rarified atmosphere, just that we liked putting two fingers up to the order of things.

Apart from our intrusions, the Lounge was exclusively the haunt of lower-middle and middle classes - or those who liked to be seen as such. It was the province of bookmakers, factory foremen, shop assistants, clerks and other white-collar workers, particularly car dealers. Of course, there were many pubs in the rougher areas where the Lounge was just as dodgy as the Public. There were no class barriers, but you had to be prepared to share the bar with some rough, hard-looking and often scarred characters – and that was just the women.

Credit Memories of Bygone Portsmouth

Family Fortunes

Though having the tallest of local family trees on my mother's side, I, like so many Portmuthians am the son of a man from another part of the Kingdom.

Born in the slums of Glasgow's Gorbals in 1915, my dad would be in some people's eyes, a stereotypical Scot. With Irish ancestry, he liked to drink and sing and was not averse to a fight if challenged or offended. He enjoyed a bet and a joke, but could be dour and sometimes fly into a sudden rage. The storm was always fleeting, and afterwards he would be surprised that anyone would remain upset by his outburst. I am sure he never laid a finger on my mother, and there was no doubt who steered the ship through the sometimes-stormy waters of their more than sixty years of marriage. I remember one or two occasions when the drink was in him and his dinner would decorate the wall, but that was as far as it ever went.

Most of all, I remember my dad's wonderful tenor voice, and how it would enchant everyone in earshot.

When employed, my dad was a good and willing worker. He could turn his hand to any activity which required no special skill, and after leaving the Navy worked as a labourer and lorry driver, door-to-door salesman, baker's roundsman and milkman.

He was a big man in both senses of the word, and especially so in physical terms. By the time he was a teenager he was nearly 6ft 5 inches, which was a giant for those times, especially in the slums of Maryhill.

In later life when the family became financially secure, he had a presence to match his size. He was hugely intelligent and bitterly resented not having had much of an education. Growing old, he mellowed to become more reflective and thoughtful and was perhaps the wisest man I have ever known. As I can now see, for most of his life he lacked confidence in himself, and my mother said this was because his mother had knocked it out of him.

Granny Kelly was the grand-daughter of an itinerant salesman (or tinker as Mother liked to say) who fled the Irish Potato Famine. Florrie Kelly grew up in a 'back-to-back' tenement in the notorious Gorbals where a floor's worth of families shared a single toilet and tap. She was a large lady and of striking appearance with an explosion of red hair and a decidedly pugnacious appearance and attitude. Unlike my father, she didn't mellow with age. In her youth she worked as a barmaid - and occasionally (again according to Mother) as a bouncer - in some of the most notorious pubs, and was said to fight like a man and even enjoy a good scrap. Her husband and my dad's father was John Wood Young, a Glasgow tram driver descended from a 16th - century gang of Border Reivers. According to which story you prefer to believe, he was killed in the Great War or kicked out by Granny Kelly when she met an English sailor who took her fancy. Albert East was almost a match for Fiery Florrie, and had run away from a family of drunken brewers in Burton-on-Trent at thirteen to join a travelling fair. He later proved his worth in the boxing booth. Anyone who could knock him down would win a fiver, but from what I heard, not many did. To avoid confusion and public censure (remember it was the 1920s), the new Mrs East changed my father's name to hers. Then in a remarkable coincidence, the family moved down from Glasgow to a house in Glasgow Road, Milton when my step-grand-father was to join HMS Glasgow. Although he loved learning, my dad was made to leave school early and get a job to contribute to the family finances.

~

Meanwhile, Mother was growing up a mile or so away in what today's estate agents like to call Eastney Village because it helps put the property prices up.

Kathleen Margaret Pitt had been born into a relatively wealthy family with long-time ties to the Royal Marines. The family history in and connections with Portsmouth had begun at the end of the 18th century when Tom Pitt walked from the village of Southwick and over Portsdown Hill to join Nelson's Navy.

Old Tom's grandson (Young Tom) had a thirst for adventure and lied about his age to sign up with the Royal Marines and fight in the Crimean War. He survived the filth, disease, incompetent leadership and furious fighting, and his campaign medal is on show in the Naval Base. He lived to the grand old age of 94 and had the last gun carriage funeral in Portsmouth in 1926.

The next generation of Pitts proved to be resourceful and - like Mother - good at seeing and cashing-in on a business opportunity. The family owned two shops in Eastney, both aimed primarily at trade from the nearby RM barracks. In one, locals and hungry bootnecks could buy a pie or pig's knuckle and a dollop of pease pudding. Next door was the family's second-hand clothing shop. The main business came from newly-joined Marines who would sell their civilian clothing for a few shillings beer money. When they left the service they could buy someone else's suit from the same place. Given the Pitt family tradition I sometimes think I let the family down by not joining the soldiers of the sea, but at least I was a

Royal Marine cadet for a short while. And in any case, in my day bootnecks and matelots were for fighting, not mixing with and especially not joining up with.

~

Over the years, the Pitt family prospered, then with some unwise investments and the Great Depression came disaster.

One afternoon, my mother came home to find her grandfather with his head in the gas oven. He had killed himself in despair after, as he saw it, failing his family by losing all his money and property.

Suddenly, Kathleen Pitt had gone from a comfortable and even privileged life to that of a poor and homeless young woman. She found a bedsit and a job in the local Twilfit corset factory and had a constant battle to make ends meet. Then, one day she met a very tall and handsome man with a beautiful voice, a very shabby mackintosh and a greyhound on a string, and I am the result.

Mother always said that the shock of the reversal of the family fortunes and her early hard times with my dad made her permanently insecure and fearful of being on the street. This is why she devoted most of her adult life to making money and stowing as much as possible away for future rainy days. In the way capricious genes work, my brother inherited her attitude to business and gift for seeing an opportunity and cashing in on it. Unfortunately for my family and their inheritance prospects, I followed my dad's carefree unconcern about where the next pound was coming from. It is an attitude I - if not my dear wife and children - often regret.

Crimean War veteran: 'Young' Tom Pitt and family

My dad with his mother, grandmother and younger brother

Family weddings: A grand affair for dad's brother Bert and Portsmouth Registry Office for my auntie Jill. Note the bicycle for the official wedding transport

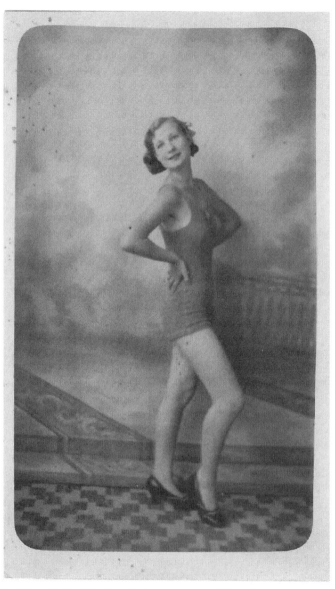

Bathing Belle: Mother before entering Miss Southsea 1937

Home Cooking

Throughout my time at Cottage Grove, my mother insisted I came home for a proper meal at dinner time. I think this was not so much that she had any criticism of school meals as that she would be failing in her duty as a mother to allow me to queue up with children who might be from poor homes.

I remember my disappointment at not seeing and trying what lay inside the big metal containers delivered each day to be served by red-faced ladies with huge, dimpled forearms. It meant I was excluded from the joys of Flies on an Island and Spam Fritters, but the consolation was I got to regularly eat the best chips in the world.

A solid and capable if not imaginative cook (few mothers were in those days) Mother would have a fixed roster for my and any full-board lodgers' midday meal; my favourite day was when corned beef and chips was the dish of the day. Thick slices would be carved from the enormous block at the local butcher's shop, served up with great, fat chips cooked in the dripping from a hundred Sunday joints. I can't recall the chip pan being emptied or cleaned out in the years we were at Castle Road; it was just topped up with the juice and drippings from the weekly roast. This gave an interesting texture, with the dripping riddled with black, crunchy nuggety remnants of past meals. I only realised how slim and smooth the chips and how brilliantly white the white of a fried egg could be when a family celebration was marked by a special meal at a Black Cat restaurant.

~

This was of course many years before the taste for exotic 'foreign' foods like pizza and hamburgers and fried chicken arrived, and at a time when garlic was only used to keep vampires at bay. People had larders but not refrigerators, let alone freezers. Housewives bought fresh supplies daily, and foods with a short shelf life like milk and cheese and butter (or more likely margarine) were kept in the larder. Big, posher houses would have larders the size of a walk-in wardrobe with a mesh-covered window to help keep the contents cool. More humble abodes made do with a box the size of a modern microwave, set in a wall. The side exposed to the yard would be punched full of holes too small for a fly to gain entry, while the door side opened into the kitchen. Milk bottles would be stood in pudding basin filled with water. These aids were not much help in high summer, so housewives had to buy thoughtfully.

Rationing, attitudes and the limited range of available foodstuffs (some items were still on ration in 1953) meant that the weekly menu would vary little from house to house. Most people in any street were on a similar, single income, and had the same in-bred tastes for what went on their plates. Nowadays, it is all about being different and following passing fancies for avocados with nigella seed and mango 'jus' for breakfast and trying to outdo the neighbours in exotic consumption. In our time we were quite happy to be the same as everyone else, and especially happy just to see food on the plate. The Green Lady would look benevolently down from most parlour walls, while a flight of carefully arranged plaster ducks would soar over the mantlepiece of the living room. It felt comfortable to be like others.

Meals were as predictable as décor, and there was a certain sense of comfort and security in knowing what was to come every day. People were still recovering from a time when they couldn't be sure they would have a roof above their heads, let alone a meal cooking in the kitchen.

It was almost enshrined in law that Sunday was the day of roast as well as rest. I can remember walking down Castle Road at midday and pausing to savour the unmistakable fragrance at each doorway. In every oven would be potatoes roasting in dripping and any combination of parsnips or sprouts or carrots, cauliflower or whatever was in season. Back then we didn't need to be encouraged to eat our five portions a day of vegetables. They were cheap and plentiful and filling.

It may be false, but my memory tells me that most families in our road could stretch to a roast Sunday dinner. In the more affluent premises it would be lamb or pork or even a rib of beef. In the less well-off homes, it might be inferior cuts, or if times were really hard, faggots or 'savoury' (i.e. meatless) sausages.

Monday was a favourite day, as the evening meal would always be bubble and squeak, using up the leftover vegetables by mashing them together and frying the result in the dripping from the roast meat.

On Tuesday it might be mashed potato and any cold meat remaining from the roast, and midweek could be a soup made up from the bones and fat from Sunday's feast. In winter, the soup or thick stew would be augmented with great, fluffy dumplings. If the roast had been lamb, my mother might simmer the bone and shreds of meat in a pan with onion, carrot and pearl barley to thicken it up. Sometimes she would overdo the pearl barley and make it more like porridge than broth.

Other main meal regulars were cottage pie, steak and kidney pudding and bangers and mash. We called sausages 'bangers' because the skin would be made of pigs' intestines which would split and disgorge the contents if the pan was made really hot. This was often a deliberate procedure, as the burned, knobbly bits at the ends were delicious. Gravy was a mainstay to accompany any even remotely suitable dish, with the exception of salad and fish. It had to be thick and 'meaty' and would be made from a combination of flour and the juices from the Sunday roast. For some reason, thin gravy was seen as a mark of stinginess, which meant you could almost stand a spoon up in ours. Although not to everyone's taste, I was genuinely fond of Spam ('luncheon meat' as it was known) fritters, but was born too late to find out what whale meat tasted like. From what I hear, I had a lucky escape. The old pun 'Whale Meat Again' was still in vogue, but you would have to know about the wartime hit by the wonderful Vera Lynn to get it.

Cockles and winkles and whelks were popular snacks in a seaside town, but fish dishes were a rarity. I think this was more an example of cultural attitudes of the time than of availability.

In a complete reversal of modern times, fish was cheap and plentiful, and to many housewives, serving it as a main meal was an admission of budgetary mismanagement. There was also a distant echo of sectarianism, as Roman Catholics were obliged to eat fish on Friday.

Fish was widely seen, as my very Protestant Scottish granny would say, as 'puir (poor) folk and invalid's food', but there were exceptions. Pilchards with salad was popular for Sunday tea, and in the event of ill-health, Mother would steam a slice of haddock and serve it to the patient with mashed potato and a knob of butter and a poached egg on top.

A definite no-no in our house was a takeaway fish-and-chip supper. It was fine for us kids to buy a thrupenny bag of chips and eat it on the way home, but serving up food someone else had cooked would be seen by Mother as an expensive indulgence.

~

Though my dad was normally barred from cooking, he was allowed in the kitchen to perform functions which

Mother would see as suitable for a male...or that a man could be trusted to perform. One of these would be the monthly toffee-apple-making ceremony. This would involve complicated (or perhaps dad just made them look complicated) manoeuvres with a saucepan and water, sugar, treacle, and curiously, a splash of vinegar. At the same time he would be blanching then spearing the apples with wooden skewers. Watching him twirl the apples in the saucepan and deftly place them upside down on the window ledge was like regarding an especially enthusiastic conductor bringing in elements of his orchestra at precisely the right time.

Another of my father's specialities was making ice lollies. It was a small drawback that we had no freezer so they could only be made in the depths of winter. The trick was to put the tea-cup moulds on the window ledge in the yard and I still remember how teeth-tingling sweet and welcome they were.

Another sweet treat was a stick of rhubarb to dip in a bag of sugar when out with my gang.

After the mammoth weekly effort of making roast dinner and five veg for the family and any visitors or lodgers invited to table, my mum would look forward to putting her feet up in the evening. This was about the only time I saw her sit still for more than ten minutes, and even then she would be doing something useful. The radio would be switched on, and Mother would occupy herself with knitting, darning or going through the household accounts while dad performed the Camp Coffee Ceremony. This beverage was a strange and syrupy blend of coffee, chicory and sugar, allegedly invented in Scotland in the late 19th century for the Gordon Highlanders to take on foreign campaigns. I remember being fascinated by the label, which showed an Indian servant with a big turban serving a seated and kilted officer. I was surprised to hear recently that Camp Coffee is still on sale. It is in the same distinctive style of bottle, but in keeping with modern sensibilities the label now shows the servant sitting alongside the officer and sharing the brew-up.

On a Sunday evening, my mother would turn a Nelson's eye to dad's indulgence of boiling up a saucepan of undiluted milk for our treat. Of course, the ban did not apply to her when she was cooking with milk or making my bedtime bowl of hot milk poured over cubes of buttered, sugared bread.

It's on record that during and in the years after WWII, the average housewife got through up to double the 1500 calories a day recommended for women today. This seems strange when one considers how few overweight women there were to be seen in my childhood. Older ladies might fill out as the years passed, but not so the young and middle-aged. I suspect this may have been something to do with the sheer effort involved in running and keeping a home clean, and that nearly all women - like men - walked or rode a bicycle for long distances.

Sugar was also on ration in my early childhood, which made sweet cakes and puddings a real treat. A list of my and the nation's sweet favourites would have to include:

Apple or Rhubarb Crumble and custard

Baked apple and custard

Spotted Dick (suet pudding) with treacle (golden syrup)

Hampshire Lardy cake

Bread and Butter pudding (slices of stale bread soaked in milk and baked with sugar)

Treacle Tart

Semolina or rice pudding with a dollop of jam

suggested Menus *for a week*

	BREAKFAST	DINNER	SUPPER
Mon.	Scrambled Egg	Cold Meat and Salad Jam Roly-Poly	Welsh Rarebit
Tues.	Bacon and Tomatoes	Baked Stuffed Haddock Jacket Potatoes Cauliflower Apple Pie and Custard	Potato Soup Cornish Pasty
Wed.	Fish Cakes	Baked Rabbit Braised Onions Baked Sliced Potatoes Macaroni Pudding Stewed Fruit	Savoury Omelet
Thurs.	Grilled Bacon and Potato Slices	Grilled Sausages Grilled Tomatoes Mashed Potato Greens Pancakes	Soused Herrings
Fri.	Porridge Anchovy Toast	Cheese and Potato Flan Sliced Carrots or Greens Marmalade Pudding	Sliced Tinned Sausages Salad
Sat.	Boiled Eggs	Mulligatawny Soup Tinned Salmon Rissoles Creamed Swedes or Carrots Mashed Potato Bread and Butter Pudding	Grilled Fish and Chipped Potatoes
Sun.	Kippers	Roast Meat Roast Potatoes Green Vegetables Yorkshire Pudding Fruit Pie and Custard	Cauliflower au gratin

NOTE.—*Serve tea or coffee at breakfast, also toast
or bread and cereals if desired.*

The Portsmouth Blitz

The translation of the German *blitz* is 'lightning'.

With the Dockyard and many other military and industrial installations, Portsmouth was inevitably a prime target for the Luftwaffe. It is estimated that 40,000 people were killed, 46,000 injured and a million homes destroyed in Britain during World War II. Portsmouth was the ninth most hit place in the country, and suffered 67 raids between July 1940 and May 1944. In that time, more than 1300 high-explosives and 38,000 incendiary bombs rained on the city. During those raids, more than a thousand citizens and service people lost their lives and more than 3000 were injured.

In property terms, nearly 7,000 homes, shops, pubs, churches, schools, a hospital and other buildings were destroyed and nearly 75,000 damaged.

For modern Portmuthians it would not be possible to imagine what it must have been like to hear the air raid sirens and know what was coming.

After one raid in 1940, many buildings around Castle Road disappeared overnight during what became known as the Portsmouth Blitz.

Unless you have seen what a cluster of high-explosive bombs can do, it is hard to imagine the scale of destruction. In place of elegant homes and long-established shops were gaping pits, filled with rubble, glass, pipes and sometimes poignant reminders that people had lived here. This made bombsites dangerous but enticing playgrounds for my generation. They were fiercely-defended meeting places for gangs, ripe for excavation in search of buried treasures, and when it snowed we would slide down the slopes on the curved, corrugated-iron roofs of Anderson air raid shelters.

Zeppelin airship bombing raids in the first World War killed hundreds, but had nowhere near the effect of the sustained and intensive bombings of World War II. It is highly unlikely that 'conventional' bombing raids will happen in the United Kingdom again, and future generations will know little about it if someone should press the button and shortcut the destruction of the planet.

Unusually for those times, Castle Road was a diverse thoroughfare in more ways than one.

In the Fifties, the inhabitants of hundreds of streets and thousands of terraced cottages would be on a similar income and lead the same sort of occupations and lives.

Credit Memories of Bygone Portsmouth

Castle Road was, for a young and ever-curious boy, intriguingly different from the norm. Our neighbours on one side were a mad woman and her daughter. Perhaps Mrs Meadows had suffered tragedy and lost a husband or child in the war, or perhaps she was just mentally deranged. In those days and unless you were so disturbed you would qualify for restrained residence in places like St James's Lunatic Asylum, people with quite severe mental disorders would often be left to look after themselves.

Poor, mad Mrs Meadows would shout abuse and chant spells and curses over the garden wall, and encourage her equally disturbed daughter to throw handfuls of vomit, cat, dog and even her own turds into our yard. She also developed an obsessive hatred for our cat Tiger, who appeared in the scullery one morning in agony with a six-inch nail through his back leg. As there was no man in the Meadows household to have a word with, there was nothing my mother and father could do but put up with living literally next door to a madhouse.

Living on the other side were, in comparison, perfect neighbours. The Smiths were a noisy but jolly, friendly and large family. Like many virile men with big families, Mr Smith was small and slight. He was also completely bald but compensated with a large walrus moustache. I don't know if he worked, but I never saw him out of his indoor rig of slippers and Charlie Chaplin-esque baggy trousers held up with wide braces over the top half of his long john underwear. His wife was as tall and wide as he was small, and clearly the head of the household. The children were mostly girls, so of no interest to me as playmates and didn't, of course, qualify for membership of our gang.

Mrs Smith was an apparently normal and sensible woman, but clearly obsessive about her children's bowel motions. In those days that was not uncommon. Parents kept a regular check on their children's visits to the toilet, and many took active steps to keep them, as they would say, 'regular'. Some, like Mrs Smith, took it to extreme and sometimes painful levels.

I remember arriving one afternoon to find the Smith children lined up in front of the fire in the living room. They looked nervous but resigned and stood with shorts down and skirts lifted. From their expressions I could tell Mrs Smith had been administering doses of the cure-all mixture of sugar syrup and sulphur tablets, known as Brimstone and Treacle. This dramatic-sounding concoction had its roots in Victorian times but was still around in the middle of the 20th century.

After the dosing by mouth it was time for the grand finale, and I remember shutting my eyes and wincing as Mrs Smith passed along the line, shoving a fingerful of Vaseline up each of her children's bottoms.

Though not overly concerned with bowel motions, my mother was an enthusiastic home medic. I was what was known then as a 'chesty' child, which required a variety of sometimes bizarre treatments. The most common-sensical was vigorous massaging of my chest with Vic Vapour Rub, and I spent more than my share of time with my head under a tea towel breathing in the steamy fumes rising from a pudding basin.

At that time the NHS was relatively new. A doctor's visit had been a costly drain on family finances in the past, so home doctoring was still the norm. There was usually a traditional treatment, though not all were based on sound scientific principles.

Some home-grown treatments would seem bizarre nowadays, but surprisingly often worked. Or appeared to. I think like homeopathy and Voodoo, belief may have been the key.

Great store was set by poultices, which were sticky concoctions applied to various parts of the body. Pancakes of mouldy bread were used to 'draw out' anything from serious infections to splinters or the contents of boils. Boils seemed as common as colds amongst children in those days, which may have been something to do with our standards of personal hygiene or choice of playgrounds.

Of the 'traditional' nostrums, there was a sort of scientific logic to the bread poultice as a natural antibiotic as the mould contained penicillin. Other ingredients included oatmeal, onion, potato and even turnip. Mustard poultices were believed to relieve colds, sprains and muscle aches, arthritis and it was thought that the scent could relieve nasal congestion.

The use of medicinal clay goes back to prehistoric times and a bottle of Kaolin and Morphine solution was always on hand in most households. It was used to help cure diarrhoea and other stomach upsets and the chalky taste was, it was said, quite addictive. For extra effectivity, a poultice for the chest to draw out a cold would be heated to almost scalding levels in the oven before application.

There were many even less scientific cures for minor ailments. Hiccups could be cured by drinking from the 'wrong' side of a glass of water. Or you might be advised to sing and dance loudly, or firmly pull your tongue out and hold it for a minute. Or a sudden shock could cause a sharp intake of breath and stop the problem, even if it did risk a heart attack or seizure for an older sufferer. Nose bleeds seemed more commonplace then, and the accepted treatment was a key or cold spoon on a piece of string lowered down inside your vest to rest in the middle of your back. Salt-water gargles for sore throats was a standard treatment, and a more unusual one was a sock with an onion in it tied loosely round the throat.

As well as cleaning windows, vinegar was a great nostrum and apple vinegar was said to cure or relieve varicose veins. Styes seemed more common then, and my mother's cure was to gently rub the affected area with her wedding ring. Surprisingly, it worked. Another offbeat treatment for constipation was to shove basil leaves up one's bottom. I never saw Mrs Smith try this solution, but that was probably because fresh basil was in short supply in the average backyard.

~

I can't remember sickness being a regular visitor to our house, but that was at least partly because my mother did not believe in being ill. I suspect our generation escaped the traumas and ill-effects of a lot of modern illnesses because we didn't know about them. Or perhaps parents were more concerned about the truly dread diseases of the time like tuberculosis and poliomyelitis. For day-to-day medicating, anything that resulted in an upset stomach or chill or even a mild fever was put down as a 'bilious attack' and treated accordingly. When I contracted impetigo after a marbles session by a drain, Mother referred to the Home Doctor manual, treated the scabs with calamine lotion and knitted me a pair of boxing glove-like mittens so I wouldn't be able to pick at them in the night.

I prized the rare occasions when I was confined to bed (or allowed to be confined to bed) with an illness as it meant even more indulgent treatment. Comics, hot drinks, traditional remedies, sweets and fruit would be delivered to my room as I lay on my bed of pain. If I could really ham it up, I'd be fed with bread and milk and brown sugar from a bowl as I lay moaning softly.

Given our situation and attitudes, accidents were common; in those days Health & Safety officers and regulations were thin on the ground.

I can remember falling through a hole into the crypt at the bombed-out church in Elm Grove and being winched out still fairly intact. My reward in convalescence was a packet of monkey nuts and a whole bottle of dandelion and burdock Corona* to myself.

In the same church on another day, Tinker Jackson took a swing with a length of pipe at a wall and hadn't realised I was standing behind him. When I didn't respond to enquiries as to whether I was still alive, I was picked up carried senseless to the nearby Timothy Whites and Taylor. Later to become a national and household name, the company was started in Portsmouth in the mid-nineteenth century, and specialised as a treatment centre for cases not serious enough for a hospital visit. Mother found me sitting on the counter with a lollipop and a bandage turban. As she said, it was lucky the pipe hit me on the head.

Playing with fire was a regular diversion, and as a curious child I liked conducting experiments involving setting things alight. A spectacular example concerned a box of Bengal matches and a length of steel tubing. Much bigger than ordinary matches, Bengal matches burned with a fierce flare-like flame, and I had wondered if they would still burn in the absence of air. To find out I stuck one end of a steel pipe into a soft patch of dirt in the back yard, lit and dropped six Bengal Matches into the other and clamped my hand over the open end. When I took my hand away, the matches were still indeed burning and erupted from the pipe, sticking to my palm. I kept all my fingers, but bear the scars still, and that put an end to my experimenting for at least a month.

I don't know the comparative statistics for childhood accidents and deaths then and now, but credit must be due to the patron saint of naughty boys in the 1950s. As far as I remember, my friends and I came mostly intact through those happy years of careless adventures on bombsites, climbing piers, going out to sea on a leaky tyre innertube and excavating for unexploded bombs.

In those days, Corona was not a merciless pandemic but a popular fizzy drink.

~

A few doors beyond the Smiths lived two brothers who my mother was more than pleased for me to have as friends.

Christopher and Robin Fitzgerald lived nearby but in another world. Their father was an RN Commander, and their mother a jolly, kind and very down-to-earth middle-class lady who stole my heart from our first meeting.

The family's house was as different from ours as our backgrounds and probable futures. There were no lodgers, and the Fitzgeralds had a room just for eating breakfast in. Even more alien was that the table was laid with place mats and damask napkins, kept in shape by silver rings. No Green Ladies or flying ducks on those walls, but sophisticated works of modern art in narrow frames.

Thick, exotic and shop-bought rugs sat smugly on

highly polished wooden parquet flooring. There was a writing bureau in the front room, and the boys even had a room of their own. In it was a wind-up gramophone and a library of children's music on fragile 78rpm discs. To me, being able to select and hear your own choice of music rather than wait for it to come up on the radio was almost science fiction. I'd spend hours in their playroom, putting in new needles and carefully dropping the arm into the groove to listen to *The Runaway Train* and *Peter and the Wolf*. Then I climbed the stairs one day to hear the surging, syncopation of *Bad Penny Blues* by Humphrey Lyttleton and knew that, whatever else, my future must include modern, swinging music with a beat.

~

Although the most liberal and informal of people, Mrs Fitzgerald was as interested in her sons' bowel motions as the other mothers in Castle Road. On the back of the toilet door was a notepad and a pencil on a string. With it, the boys were charged to register the date, time, type and consistency of the result of their visit.

On the plus side for me, there were air rifle sessions in the garden and soccer and cricket sessions with real bats and balls. I was often invited to tea and I remember one occasion when our different worlds were made real. After home-made manor cake and strangely aromatic tea, Mrs Fitzgerald spread a slice of toast with what I took to be blackberry jam. She presented me with a corner as if offering a special treat, then watched in anticipation as I bit into it. Instead of fruity sweetness I got a mouthful of rank fishiness.

'Yech,' I said with the forwardness of childhood, 'the jam's gone bad.'

She smiled and explained that the jam was something called caviar, which some people quite liked.

This small epiphany neatly summed up the difference

between our households and lives to come. Before they went off to exclusive prep and boarding schools and distinguished careers in the Law, Christopher and Robin and I shared the same adventures on bomb sites and beach and were very close chums. But I knew at the time that there was no future in our friendship when childhood's days were done.

~

Living not far from but at the very opposite end of the social spectrum from the Fitzgeralds were the O'Kellys.

The brood was said to number more than twenty, but that was hard to confirm as they were never seen together at the same time. It was said by some unkind people that they couldn't go out *en masse* as there were less shoes in the house than feet to wear them.

The boisterous, noisy, mischievous and, surprisingly happy family lived in a very decrepit and distressed property in a street off Castle Road. Virtually the whole block had been laid waste by air raids, but ironically the O'Kelly tumbledown home had survived.

Two of the boys of around my age were associate members of our gang, though I was sensible enough not to invite Archie or Alfie to meet Mother. Like most mothers in the immediate area, mine would rather I did not become too close to the O'Kelly children. Her feelings were, I think, part snobbery, but also the fear that any close contact would bring the spectre and prospect of poverty too close for comfort.

But to me, the differences between the O'Kelly children and my easy life was a fascination. I was reminded many years later of Mother coming in to my room to kiss me goodnight and finding me lying on the floor, covered with coats that had been hanging in the hall. When she asked me what I was doing, I said I wanted to sleep like the O'Kellys.

On another occasion Mother found a cake and a meat pie missing from the larder. When pushed, I admitted I had given them to Archie O'Kelly as he had said the family were dining on bread and pull-it* that evening. I can still see her face and opposing emotions, and how she took me in her arms and said I was a good and thoughtful boy, but had to learn that charity must always begin at home.

~

Perhaps because of the time spent adventuring outdoors, most boys belonged to a gang, often with a silly name. In those days, boys' gangs traded in cigarette cards and marbles rather than drugs and were just groups of friends who lived near to each other. There were some unwritten rules, and each gang would have its own territory, bombsite and carol-singing and bonfire night preserves which were generally respected. There would be some trespassing and filching of bonfire wood and bomb shrapnel as trophies, but I don't remember a single case of violence between gangs. That came in later years.

Predictably, our gang was known - probably only to us - as the Castle Road Knights. Officially, membership was limited to residents of the road, but schoolmates or friends from further afield could become associate members.

I naturally appointed myself as the leader, and my deputies were Melvin Townsend and Cyril Scott, who lived on the other side of the road. Living a few doors along and directly opposite our house, Tommy Horner was our secretary and communications officer. Officially, this meant he kept the minutes of meetings about our monitoring of suspected local spies and Bolsheviks, using a notepad with a box of matches stuck to the cover for use if there was a risk of it falling into the wrong hands.

Also in the spirit of our fictional heroes, each night at bedtime we would exchange coded messages by torch. The problem was that the only Morse code we knew was for S.O.S., so we had devised a basic system of one flash for A, two for B and so on up to 26 for Z. As there was no way of indicating punctuation or gaps between words, It wasn't an effective system and we usually gave up after ten minutes before climbing into bed with the week's copy of *The Dandy, Beano* or *Wizard.*

In those hard times, families often had no more than a loaf of bread to keep them going. A chicken would have seemed like manna from Heaven. It thus became a grim joke that their evening meal would consist of 'bread and pull-it', rather than a tasty pullet.

In a time before electronic games and smart phones, weekly comics were a hugely popular source of diversion and entertainment.

Interestingly, British comics featured not superheroes but ordinary though in some ways extraordinary people we could admire or identify with. One of the hundreds of titles produced by DC Thomson, *The Dandy* was launched in 1937 and lasted until 2012. Regular characters were Keyhole Kate, Hungry Horace and my favourite, Desperate Dan. He was an urban cowboy who was also the strongest man in the world. Dan was so tough he had to remove the bristles from his massive jaw with a blowtorch. In spite of his fearsome appearance, he was a good-hearted and amiable soul, if of limited intelligence. His favourite meal was an enormous cow pie, served complete with horns, and for many decades his name was used to describe anyone with an oversized chin.

Most boys were lucky to have one comic a week; thanks to my over-indulgent mother, I had several.

As the name suggested, *Film Fun* featured the adventures of movie stars, many from a previous era. Along with the serialised adventures of cowboy stars like Roy Rogers, comedic heroes like Charlie Chaplin, Buster Keaton, Laurel and Hardy, Abbot and Costello and W.C. Fields would get in and sometimes out of scrapes every week.

I was, of course, only interested in boy's comics and male characters, but there were exceptions like Beryl the Peril and Minnie the Minx. They were what we used to call 'tomboys' and, as far as I was concerned, tough enough to be honorary males. There was a weekly publication called *Girl*, featuring heroines like Anne the

Air Hostess and Belle of the Ballet, but for a boy to be seen even looking inside the cover would have invited ridicule.

~

Of all the comics, probably the most popular was *The Beano*. The first edition came out in 1938 and the title is still going strong. In its heyday in the 1950s *The Beano* sold a staggering two million copies a week.

Its success was based on the attraction of the regular characters, who included Dennis the Menace and his dog Gnasher, The Bash Street Kids, Minnie, the Minx, Lord Snooty, Biffo the Bear and Roger the Dodger. It is interesting that, in those post-war years, the running theme of the strips was of the young characters causing and getting into trouble and then either escaping or suffering retribution in the form of a cane-swishing teacher or belt-swinging father. Physical punishment was permissible then and, as even we victims agreed, fair enough. In all the comics there would be lots of ill-thought-out schemes, painful accidents and outcomes, but all the characters had good hearts and intentions.

Aimed at an older readership *The Hotspur* and *Wizard* were the two leading 'story papers'. This meant they also featured written adventures, typically about lantern-jawed, heroic (and always white) British men. One of my favourite characters was *The Wolf of Kabul*, or Second Lieutenant Bill Samson, a British Intelligence agent working undercover on the North-West frontier. He was armed only with two daggers, which were frequently 'red with blood to the hilt'. His faithful servant was Chung, who crushed heads by the dozen with his cricket bat, or as he called it, his 'clicky-ba.'

Amongst other heroes was *Wilson the Wonder Athlete*, born in the 18th century but maintaining such a rigorous fitness regime that he lived to fight in the First World

War. Then there was *V for Vengeance*, featuring the Deathless Men. They were a band of masked concentration camp escapees who had been horribly tortured and spent their time tracking down and exacting usually terrible revenge on their former captors.

Being less than a decade after the end of hostilities, heroic Brits knocking the stuffing out of evil Krauts was a popular theme. The German soldiers were pictured as scowling, brawny, extremely ugly types who cursed a lot in a mixture of mangled English and *faux*-German ('Donner und Blitzen! You are going to die, Tommy!') before being knocked off by a cheeky Cockney squaddie.

Then there was *The Eagle*, which was required reading for boys with an interest in technology and science fiction. It was first published in April 1950 and was an instant and huge success. The star characters were Dan Dare, Pilot of the Future and his evil enemy The Mekon. He was a weedy alien with an enormous head who floated around on what looked like half a giant snooker ball. Other popular strips were *Riders of the Range*, and *PC 49*. A big favourite was the regular diagrammatic feature which stripped down and revealed the workings of a modern engineering achievement like the de Havilland Comet jet plane.

Prizes for All

The Fifties saw an explosion of gifts or 'prizes' aimed at children to influence their choice of comic or to get them to nag their parents to buy a particular brand of breakfast cereal.

In comics, a regular freebie would be a particularly noisy and therefore popular device. It was a hinged triangle of cardboard with a folded piece of brown paper glued inside. You 'loaded' the paper into the triangle, crept up behind someone (usually a girl) and brought it down sharply as if cracking a whip. Thanks to a scientific principle of which I am still unaware, the brown paper snapped out with a really satisfying and surprisingly loud bang.

The 'prizes' in breakfast cereal boxes were quite often surprisingly inventive and always much sought-after. I particularly remember a series of plastic space troopers with detachable helmets, and a working submarine to be found in a box of Kellogg's Corn Flakes in 1954. You put a pinch of baking powder in a compartment and let the tiny sub sink to the bottom of the bath. The powder would react to the water, bubbles would appear and the submarine would miraculously rise to the surface. Along the same lines were divers that rose and sank and sharks with moving tails which were powered by elastic bands. Most mystifying of all was the magnetised 'King Tut' mummy which would not stay in its sarcophagus unless you knew the trick.

These distractions and games might not seem very exciting to younger readers, but as I constantly point out in this book, you mostly had to make your own entertainment in those distant, post-war years. It also helped that we had found it was best to be easily pleased.

An early summer afternoon. School is done for the day and we are reclining on the coal bunker in Tinker Jackson's back yard.

Tinker lives in one of the dozens of identical streets near Cottage Grove, running off Somers Road. He is an associate member of the Castle Road gang, and was what was then known as a bit of a rascal. To be fair, I don't think he tried to cause trouble; it's just that when it came, he was liable to be close to hand.

Tinker and I have been talking about Samantha Stott's front bottom, how strange girls are, and trying to work out what was so funny about the God Save The Queen joke. Tinker says he has it on good authority from one of the Big Boys that the joke is about what the Duke of Edinburgh will have to do with his willy to make a baby come out of Her Majesty's tummy. I say his informant must have been making it up as everyone knows that mothers buy their babies from their local hospital.

Tinker doesn't know who his mother or father are or where they are, and pretends he doesn't care. He lives with his auntie Nancy half-way down Henrietta Street, in a rented two-up-and-two-down terraced house. Inside and out it is just like hundreds of others in the area, and thousands throughout the City.

In no more than twenty years the monstrous tower blocks of Somerstown will sprout from this spot and Portsmouth would become a different place. But in 1953 there was a comforting uniformity to areas and the properties and the people who lived in them. Henrietta Street is long gone, replaced in the 1970s by the Somerstown estate, a grim mix of high- and low-rise buildings. They must be luxurious inside compared to the homes they replaced, but I doubt the present residents appreciate how lucky they are.

In our days we were all known to the local beat bobby, but only in the way he knew every family and every family member on his patch. Soon enough, drugs would be bought and sold like sweets, violent crime would rocket and technology and a ceaseless development programme would make Portsmouth a different place.

But on that long summer's day in 1953, we didn't know or much care about what was to come, and sat on the coal bunker waving to friends and neighbours in their back yards and feeling part of the fabric of the community. Nowadays every race, religion or sexual orientation has its own 'community', but then it quite properly meant the people you lived with and near. As I have said, it was the sameness rather than the differences that made the people of Portsmouth feel at home in their skins.   Inside and out, the houses emphasised that sameness.

Looking across the low walls, a row of near-identical backyards stretched into the distance. Each would have a coal bunker just like the one we were sitting on. All walls would be whitewashed, and a zinc bath would be hanging from a six-inch nail driven into the scullery wall. Alongside the bath would be the outside toilet (not that there was an inside one) in which a wad of neatly torn squares of newspaper would be ready for use. Some might offer proper rolls of cheap 'bum sandpaper' if the residents could afford it - or had access to an alternative supply chain. Some might be marked as the Property of British Rail. Long before the days of the Andrex puppy, Izal was a creation of harsh, thin paper impregnated with the disinfectant of the same name. During the war, some had been stamped with the face of Adolf Hitler.

Entering any one of ten thousand flat-fronted, terraced cottages, the visitor would step over the threshold into a dank, dark, narrow passageway. Up to waist height and masking the standard rising damp would be a thick, embossed paper known as Lincrusta. There were two general choices of colour: Windsor soup brown or a virulent shade of green. The floor in the passageway would be covered with linoleum, often made up of off-cuts with the joins disguised by rugs made from rags or woollen tufts. Nowadays, making tufted rugs is an expensive hobby; then it was a chore usually shared by the children.

Depending on the size of the family, the front room or parlour would be kept for best or used as a bedroom. If a best room, it would be filled with the furniture considered too good for everyday use.

A stairway would be found a little way along the usually dank, dark passageway. With no room for the more gentle rise of a return staircase, it would be more like a stepladder, with the landing leading off to the two bedrooms.

At the end of the passageway would be the door to the combined living room and kitchen, becoming a bathroom when the zinc tub was pulled in from the yard to the lean-to scullery. The kitchen corner area would usually feature a row of shelves and a tall, narrow cabinet with a hinged flap which would act as a preparation surface. Nearly all houses had a gas cooker by then, though I knew of some poorer households that still used an old range or even open fire. This room was where meals were eaten and cooked and the family gathered in the evenings. Unlike today, being sent to your room then was a punishment.

As well as humans, the kitchen would be home to a mouse family, which is why nearly every household had a cat. If the occupiers couldn't afford a mouser, they could always borrow or temporarily steal one.

Nowadays all the seating points at the television. Then, there would be a couple of armchairs in pole position in front of the fireplace, while children shared the table.

Some houses might have squeezed an upright piano into the front of the living room, but generally the main source of entertainment was the radio, or as we would have called it, the wireless.

In these days of plug-in fragrance dispensers and a lust for ultimate hygiene, the 1950s dwelling with its dark corners and permanent aroma of cabbage and socks and bodies would be a house of horror; for millions it was a place of comfort and refuge after a hard day's work.

~

Even though he had no real family and I came from such a secure and loving home, a part of me envied Tinker Jackson.

He didn't seem to worry about anything, and was popular and sometimes feared by other boys. Thinking back, I realise he was truly a free spirit, and I hope he's having or had a good life.

Meeting him on the way home from school on a long-ago day, I realised I had another reason to be envious. He was sporting a black eye, but, more importantly, he had a dog on a length of twine.

It was of very mixed race, and missing a hind leg and at least half of one ear. I don't know if we didn't take as much care of our pets then, but three-legged dogs and cats were not uncommon. One of the boys in our year had a two-legged whippet and would charge a ha'penny to let you watch it do tricks in his back yard.

When I asked Tinker what the dog was called, he said he didn't know what its name had been, but it was now Patch. When I asked him about the black eye, he said he'd got it from one of a couple of boys he had seen throwing stones at Patch. He had seen them off, and as the dog had no collar, he'd decided to adopt it. Like his aunty was looking after him, Tinker would look after Patch and see that he had a happy life. Or at least a happier one than when he was all alone on the streets.

He let me walk Patch to his new home, and I went home feeling very sad and trying not to cry. There had not been a dog at Castle Road since Sally the wire-hair terrier had died, and it had been my fault she died a painful death. I had left the shed door open, and Sally had got in and eaten some rat poison dad had put down. Both my parents said it was not my fault and these things happened, but I cried for days with grief at her loss and anger at myself. Whatever they said, I knew it was my fault, and I still remember the pain of that remorseless guilt.

Credit JJ Marshallsay

Thanks to Air Marshall Goering, our little gang had lots of adventure playgrounds. Bombed-out churches, factories, shops and houses were a source of endless amusement.

In summer, we would sit round fires on remnants of furniture and cook lumps of dough on sticks. In winter when it snowed, we'd toboggan down the slopes into shattered basements on the curved tin roofs of Anderson shelters. At any time of year there would be the constant excavation beneath rubble and twisted pipes and shattered doors and windows in search of buried treasure. Or, we shivered to think, dead bodies or detached limbs. More likely finds would be an old photo or even a purse or pipe or other poignant reminder of the family which lived there. To us unsentimental kids, the most eagerly sought-after finds were shards of shrapnel from the bombs that had destroyed the property. If they had a Nazi marking, symbol or stamp on them, so much more the swap value.

As well as bomb-dumps, my gang had its own secret and very atmospheric meeting place. Some gangs met in derelict buildings, others in the crypts of bombed-out churches. Ours was a really high-status place. A minor problem was that we couldn't boast about it or it would no longer be secret.

Down at the seafront and between the fun fair and the roofless Garrison church was a moat and grassy embankment overlooking Spithead, the entrance to Portsmouth harbour. The embankment and moat and a few stone walls were the remains of ancient fortifications. Nowadays the area has been cleaned up and dandified to make a pleasant seating and play area with a walk through a tunnel and across a wooden bridge over the moat to the promenade. With other priorities immediately after the War, the area had been left to nature. The authorities hadn't got round to replacing the blown-off roof of the nearby Garrison church or filling in the gaps in the ancient streets of Old Portsmouth, so were not going to bother with a grassy knoll and big ditch. A now redundant storage facility for the WD, it was officially still a restricted area and off-limits to civilians. This made it a challenge the Castle Road Knights could not ignore.

The entrance to the tunnel on the landward side of the embankment was a barbed wire-festooned, rusty metal gate. The *tunnel ended on the other side of the embankment as an opening thirty feet above the junk and rubble-littered moat. The seaward opening was guarded on either side by viciously-spiked railings which stuck out over the moat. To get to it, all we had to do was sneak along the grassy slope, swing out onto the railings and navigate the spikes. For bombsite habitués, this was no big deal. It meant dangling over the drop into the moat, but that was part of the fun. Clambering into the hole and passageway, we would then make our way to a brick-lined and arched room deep in the heart of the embankment. It was a dark and damp and smelly place, but the atmosphere and echoes and shadows cast by our candles made it the perfect setting for our gang HQ.

We gathered there at least once a week, always as dusk fell and usually after a day at the Sixpenny Swimming Pool or the Hot Walls, where we would play on and under the ancient pier from where Nelson had set sail for the Battle of Trafalgar. When in funds or favour at home we would take provisions, perhaps a jam or sugar or dripping sandwich (sometimes a combination of all three) and maybe some monkey nuts and chews and bags of Tony's broken crisps. Drinks would be cold tea or sherbet lemonade in an old Corona bottle.

In the suitably dramatic surroundings, we would plan

future adventures, tell made-up stories and frighten ourselves with imagined voices or movements beyond the pool of light from the candles. We also planned to seal our loyalty to each other and the gang in blood, but always forgot to bring a sharp knife.

~

Whatever we got up to and were back home not too long after dark, our parents would be unconcerned. This was quite a normal attitude, but there were exceptions. I remember a cousin of about my age arriving from the westcountry with his mother to stay for the weekend. I was charged with looking after Frederick and showing him the sights, and given a whole half-crown to spend at the fun fair. After feasting on candy floss, rock, whelks and doughnuts and enjoying a couple of near-death experiences on rickety rides, we arrived home well after dark to find his mother in near - hysterics. It had taken all Mother's persuasive powers to prevent her from calling out the Police, Fire and Lifeboat services.

Mother was deeply apologetic and gave me a bawling-out for being out so late, but she smiled a secret smile and winked when they were not looking. I think, like many Portsmouth mothers, she thought small boys were indestructible, and perhaps that helped make us so.

I learned recently that the tunnel running past our gang HQ was used by Horatio Nelson on his way to HMS Victory to set sail for Cape Trafalgar and his destiny. The great man would have walked within feet of where the Castle Road Knights held their meetings.

The Big Bang

'Remember, Remember the Fifth of November,
Gunpowder, Treason and Plot.
I see no reason why Gunpowder Treason
Should ever be Forgot...'

September, and it was back to school. The endless days of summer were past, but there was much to look forward to. Christmas was coming, but before then we would be sending Guy Fawkes up in smoke.

These were the days when Halloween was little known, let alone made such a fuss about. Nowadays, the reason for the burning in effigy of the Gunpowder Plot* ringleader Guy Fawkes has been mostly forgotten, and the event stretched from a single evening to a fortnight. It has also changed from a competition to see who could build the biggest and most potentially lethal bonfire to a competition to see how much people can spend on lighting up the night sky with spectacular displays of very conspicuous consumption.

In the reverse of today, the preparations for Guy Fawkes/Bonfire/Fireworks Night occupied us for months, while the event was strictly limited to the evening of November the 5th. That made it, like Christmas Day, all the more eagerly anticipated.

Each road or neighbourhood had its own bombsite on which to build a bonfire, and children would spend months scavenging or stealing the materials and growing theirs. With the destruction of so many properties in the Portsmouth Blitz there was no shortage of wooden beams, floorboards and rafters, remnants of carpet and linoleum and anything else remotely flammable. Then there would be boxes and crates donated by or stolen from local shopkeepers, or, even sweeter, soapbox carts pinched from rival gangs. Bonfire building became something of an obsession, and some would be bigger than the houses surrounding them. Cuts, bruises, infections and the odd broken bone would be accumulated during the building, but serious injuries were rare before the big night.

As well as sitting on top of the bonfire, the 'Guy' was also a device for raising money for fireworks. Nowadays you will see homeless people begging outside shops and in busy thoroughfares. In the Fifties it was hard to avoid the demands of small boys for a 'penny for the guy'.

The quality of the guy would vary greatly and have an obvious effect on the frequency and level of donation. At the top end would be almost life-like dummies in suits of old clothes, with gloved hands and sometimes even shoes which would be rescued before the blaze. Others would be no more than a stuffed pillow case with a face daubed on it. Unsurprisingly, Tinker Jackson and his Henrietta Street cartel always took the most money. He had an excellent patter, but what sold it was the surprisingly life-like guy. It was so real in appearance because it was actually his mate Lazy Harry. Harry was a small, shapeless boy who earned his nickname from his ability to drop off and lie still for hours on end, particularly during lessons.

~

Each gang would have its own fiercely defended pitch, and ours was by a bus stop outside Timothy White and Taylors in Elm Grove. We would harangue passers-by from after school until dark and at weekends. The level of reward varied from a near-derisive farthing to as much as a half-crown or two-bob bit from a drunken sailor or young man out to impress his lady friend. Technically we were openly begging, but even the most mean-spirited policeman would turn a blind eye unless he was in a bad mood. A good pitch, worked hard for the month leading up to Bonfire Night could bring in several pounds in coppers and silver coins, all counted, re-counted and gloated over as the tally mounted. When divvied up, a pound apiece would buy a huge armoury of fireworks, especially if you went for noise and danger rather than spectacle. A cheap banger would cost a penny and a much louder blockbuster was tuppence. Sparklers and Catherine Wheels and Fountains were for girls or cissies, but Jumping Jacks could be put to good use by dropping in the midst of a crowd. Roman Candles were meant to be stuck in the earth and shoot their miniature fireballs into the sky, but could be aimed at unwary cats and dogs, rival gang members or even mates. Rockets could also be used as projectiles by sending them off from a launcher made out of a long cardboard roll. The shooter would kneel and balance it on his shoulder, while the loader would light the blue paper and slip the rocket into the back end of the tube. He would then block the end off with a saucepan lid or gloved hand and, as seen in war films, tap the shooter on the head to let him know the weapon was primed and ready.

~

Like Christmas, Bonfire Night was agonisingly slow in coming and gone in an almost literal flash.

Our bonfire was on a big bombsite just off Castle Road and once occupied by a brewery. Seventy years on and I can recall those nights with almost total clarity. In my mind's eye I am standing in my room, cramming bangers and Bengal matches into the pockets of my grey windcheater. All tooled up, I go into the kitchen for the potatoes for baking in the fire and a couple of dad's toffee apples. Mother is knitting in the sitting room, and smiles fondly, kisses my cheek benignly and says, 'Have a lovely time, Podge.'

Arriving at the bombsite, I'd help douse the giant pyramid of tarred boards and broken furniture with a gallon of paraffin from Dipman & Malpas, and reach for the box of matches.

I don't know the nationwide casualty rate for Bonfire Night at that time, but I don't remember any of our gang or rivals being killed or even seriously wounded. We were certainly not as safety conscious then, but perhaps we were more agile.

For any readers who think that history only started with their arrival in this world, the Gunpowder Plot was a foiled attempt by English Catholics to blow up King James I at the State Opening of Parliament on November 5th, 1605. A tip-off led to the discovery of 36 barrels of gunpowder in cellars below the Palace of Westminster the day before the Opening. Guy Fawkes was arrested at the scene and he and fellow conspirators were tortured then hanged, drawn and quartered in public. The near-miss was celebrated every year with church bells and bonfires, giving generations of children the excuse to make mischief and play with fire.

"Standard," FIREWORKS

HUDDERSFIELD, ENGLAND.

TO GET THE BEST RESULTS ALWAYS FOLLOW THE
DIRECTIONS MARKED ON THE FIREWORKS

HERE ARE A FEW GOOD TIPS:—

Jumping Crackers perform their best antics on hard ground or paving.

Pin Wheels Use a strong pin fixed firmly to a post. Fix the pin to slope very slightly downwards from the post. This keeps the wheel near the head of the pin and prevents it binding against the post.

Pom-Pom Cannons The warning spurt of sparks is for 5 seconds before the bang.

Flyers or Flying Imps Stand clear when you have lit the touchpaper as they fly in any direction.

Roman Candles & Long Fountains Fix them firmly in an upright position by pushing them into soft earth.

Volcanos, Mount Vesuvius and Short Fountains Stand them on a level surface before lighting.

Air Bombs and Star Shells Fix them firmly in an upright position, clear of buildings and overhead obstructions.

Wear an old glove for those marked "to be held in the hand."

Never get over the top of a firework to light it (or after you have lit it). Light it at arms length.

"Standard Fireworks" Ltd., Huddersfield.

Peace on Earth

'While shepherds washed their socks by night,
All seated round the tub,
A bar of Sunlight Soap came down,
And they began to scrub'

(1950s schoolboy version of traditional Christmas carol)

So far, 1953 had been a very good year for us kids.

First had come the joyous news of the lifting of the sweet and chocolate rationing to help the celebrations surrounding the Coronation. Then we'd basked in a scorching summer and survived the blazes and bangers of Bonfire Night. Now, the biggest event of our year was just weeks away.

With all the other excuses to over-indulge it may be no big deal nowadays, but it's hard to exaggerate the level of anticipation and eagerness the approach of Christmas fomented. By mid-December, some children would be literally sick with excitement. For the lucky ones there would be an orgy of presents and unlimited chocolate and jelly and trifle and other sweet treats. For many, the thought of what was to come was as exciting as the actual event.

For adults it was one of the few occasions apart from weddings and funerals when everyone was encouraged to eat and drink too much…and smoke cigars instead of tailor-made or rolled-up cigarettes. Seven decades on, the smell of a burning cigar still makes me think of long-gone Christmases.

At school, end of term was always eagerly anticipated;

at Christmas time, we were whipped into a near-frenzy of festive preparation. English lessons were dropped in favour of Christmas card and decoration making. Miles of paper chains were made with strips of coloured paper made into links with flour and water paste. Simple paper lanterns were also DIY decoration favourites. For older pupils there would be Christmas cracker-making sessions, and trying to make them live up to their name with strips of sandpaper and a pinch of gunpowder often ended in minor damage or injury. Then there would be the carol singing service and nativity play rehearsals.

At home, last year's decorations would be brought down from the attic and dusted off. To go with the home-made paper chains there would be collapsible - and sometimes collapsed - paper bells and globes. There were no fairy lights, but better-off families would have a Christmas tree, decorated with cotton wool snow and real candles. Others would make do with a painted tree branch or shrub or bush from a nearby bombsite.

Sprigs of holly and mistletoe would be bought from the market at Charlotte Street or door-to-door vendors. Sometimes the callers were real or pretend gypsies. The pretend ones wore big earrings, colourful headscarves and even false moustaches in the belief that it was one of the rare times of the year when gypsy door-knockers were welcome. The proper gypsies would try and sell you clothes pegs and lucky heather, but might curse you if you didn't buy anything from them.

The shops and stores also played their part in setting the mood. Small shopkeepers would put up modest decorations and expand their lines to include once-a-year specialities, but the department stores really went to town.

Almost unimaginably lavish decorations would hang from high ceilings, while recorded carols would play non-stop through tinny loudspeakers. Toys would be on show to excite the children and worry their parents, but the real attraction for us would be the visit to Father Christmas's Grotto. Every year the top stores would strive to outdo each other in the style and theme of transport to the Grotto. There would be sleigh rides through a snowy landscape occupied by oversized elves and dwarfs, or even a rocket ship with hand painted and operated stars and planets being cranked past the portholes to create the sense of movement. At the end of the journey we would queue up to sit on the lap of a not-always jolly man in a red costume and false whiskers. Fat men were not that common then, so it was more likely to be a skinny assistant salesman with knobbly knees and a cushion up the front of his costume. If you were lucky, they would not have bad breath or a body odour problem.

~

Like the shops and stores, pubs would lay in extra supplies and exotic drinks like Advocaat, Babycham and cherry brandy. Most would have been running a Christmas Club, and pay-out night would be a big occasion. In theory, members paid in a varying amount each week to accrue a lump sum to see the family through the festive season. The system was sound, but it was not uncommon for the club secretary to abscond with all the money. During the rest of the year, landlords might run off with the barmaid. At Christmas they sometimes ran off with the Christmas Club fund; sometimes they ran off with the fund and the barmaid. On very rare occasions they ran off with the man who ran the fund.

By the start of December, children would be writing their Christmas lists and sending them to Father Christmas. This was done by holding the piece or paper over the fire, when it would magically be whisked up the chimney on its way to the North Pole. Most of us realised that it was heat rising and not magic that sent the list up the chimney, but it was important to pretend to believe that was what was happening.

~

At last, Christmas Eve would arrive, and for once children everywhere would look forward eagerly to bedtime. None were more eager than I. Although it's seven decades ago and so many memories have faded, I remember the emotions and sensations of Christmas Eve bedtime with absolute clarity.

There was the cold, crispness of the sheets as my mother tucked me in, the sensations of icy feel of the lino as I got up and ran across to the window as soon as she left. My breath would steam and there would sometimes be ice as well as condensation on the inside of the glass. Every room at our house had a fireplace, but the only one lit every day was in the kitchen-cum-living room. A fire would burn in the front room for Christmas and Boxing Day, but there was never any form of heating in the upstairs rooms. Like most managers of the family finances, Mother regarded heating bedrooms as an unjustifiable expense, as bedclothes and blankets provided enough warmth to get us through the coldest nights.

At the window for my seventh visit in an hour, I would wipe away the condensation, press my nose against the glass in the hope of seeing a distant figure zooming across the night sky. Such was the power of suggestion that I and millions of small children regularly saw unusual movements in the heavens, and if we tried really hard, hear the jingle of distant bells.

~

By ten o'clock, Mother would arrive to bribe me with a

piece of chocolate. With it there would be a Dandy or Beano album which, she always said, Father Christmas had sent ahead in case of a problem with getting to sleep. She would also remind me that he would not arrive to fill the pillow case at the foot of my bed until I was truly asleep.

Later and with the chocolate eaten and album read, I would hear the Fitzgeralds setting out for Midnight Mass. I envied the boys, not because they were Catholic, but because the family followed the German tradition of handing out the presents from around the tree early on Christmas Eve.

Eventually and despite all my efforts I'd fall asleep. On waking, I would crawl across the coverlet in the dark and feel for the pillow case. There was no greater disappointment than finding it empty, and no greater joy than finding it knobbly-edged full.

I'd try to keep to my room, but by dawn I'd be waking brother John to show him how my sonic ray gun worked and sounded. He was only four years older than me, but in those days that counted as almost a generation. As a teenager, he would have spent Christmas Eve with his mates, hanging around outside pubs and trying to look as if they had just left them if any girls of note walked by.

After annoying John, I'd make for my parents' room to show them what Father Christmas had brought. Until I accepted the awful truth, it never occurred to me that they might know exactly what had been in that bulging pillow case.

Nowadays, I think of what a strain the cost of all those presents must have put upon the family finances, and how many extra shifts of waitress work my mother must have worked to make sure my pillow case was full. I also think of all the children who must have woken up on Christmas Day with not a single present, but then it never occurred to me what a very lucky little boy I was.

The first and usually only household task for my dad on Christmas Day was to make and light the front room fire.

Mother would of course do all the organising, preparation, cooking and serving of dinner, tea and supper, and the clearing away and washing up afterwards. I believe this division of labour was the same in most homes.

In theory, men went to work during the week and brought in the wages. Women's work was looking after the family and home, which meant taking care of virtually everything from shopping and cleaning and doctoring and budget-managing to the odd bit of bricklaying or climbing on to the roof to fix a broken tile. They would usually only resort to the really physical chores in exasperation after months of nagging hadn't worked.

Along with re-soling the family shoes and doing the football pools, lighting the fire was one of the few jobs that most men saw as their province. This attitude might go back to genetic memories of prehistoric times, or perhaps husbands thought making a fire was a skill exclusive to males. Mind you, a lot of women were allowed to clean out the grate before the ceremony started - and take the ashes out and the coal in.

In the days BCH (Before Central Heating), and apart from costly and often dangerous electrical devices, the coal fire was the only form of heating. Nowadays, the whole house is kept at a comfortable temperature; then, keeping the passageway or toilet warm would have been seen as extravagance to the point of madness. All winter the only fire would be in the kitchen/living-room. Apart, that is, from Christmas and Boxing Day. By 1954, I was reckoned old enough to play an active part in the yearly ritual under dad's supervision.

First was the layer of scrunched-up balls of newspaper. Rolled too tightly and they would not catch; too loosely and they would flare up and turn to ash before setting fire to the kindling wood. These strips of wood came from broken crates and could be bought in bundles from the local shop or enterprising boys like Tinker Jackson who knocked at the door. It was generally cheaper from them, probably because they had pinched the crates.

When all the slivers of wood had been carefully positioned, little nuggets of coal would be balanced on the gaps between them, and all was ready for ignition. It was a matter of pride as well as economy that only a single match would be needed to get the fire going.

When the paper faggots were burning briskly and the smaller bits of kindling afire, it was time to increase the draught going under the grate and up the chimney. This was done by holding a double page from the local paper across the fireplace, leaving room underneath for the air to be sucked in and upwards. My dad liked to use the sports results pages so he could remind himself how much he would have won had he backed the right horse or dog. This was not a time to be distracted, as it was common for the newspaper to catch fire and disappear up the chimney. This could be a fire hazard if the flue hadn't been swept in recent years.

Larger lumps of coal would now be added, and the fire 'damped down' to gently warm the room before the guests arrived. Dad would look at me as if we had just successfully split the atom under his leadership, solemnly shake my hand and then go off to clean up and get ready for his yearly Christmas Morning tour. This would leave me free to take pot shots at the fire with my new Jet Morgan Ray-Gun Blaster, which was a water pistol by any other name. It made a satisfying sizzle when the jet hit a burning coal, but I had to be careful not to put the fire out. When I got tired of that, I'd reload my ray-gun at the scullery sink and go out in search of next-door's cat.

~

While dad was getting ready for his goodwill tour, Mother would already be hours into her preparations for feeding at least a soccer team's worth of guests. Somehow, working in a crowded and small kitchen with not much more than a four-ring gas stove and a butler sink, she would come up with a feast of roast turkey and leg of pork and at least five types of vegetables. And Christmas pudding and mince pies and custard and trifle to follow.

Then there would be the preparations to make sure nobody went hungry at tea-time, which would feature toast and jam (or dripping), baked ham and cold cuts and mince pies and cake, all of course home-made. Given her work-load, I suspect Mother would have been pleased to have my father off her hands and out of the house.

The tradition was that he and, if home from the sea, my uncle Bill would visit at least a dozen homes to pass on their seasonal wishes. The people on their list would include old friends, workmates and people who called at our house during the year to deliver milk and bread and services. Even the local bookie's runner would be visited, allowing my dad to lay a bet for the Boxing Day card at the greyhound stadium. Naturally, the callers would be invited in to take a drop of something and toast the season of goodwill. Sometimes there would be more than one drink at each house, but my dad was always back home in time to meet the guests. This was achieved because my mother gave him a deadline of an hour before they were due to arrive.

~

With greetings and wishes exchanged and coats hung up in the hall, there would be at least a dozen people squeezed in around the front room dining table. Unwanted furniture would have been moved elsewhere for the day, and mismatching chairs assembled from all rooms and friendly neighbours.

At the head of the table would be dad, acting as entertainments manager and in charge of keeping glasses topped up. Depending on how many houses they had called in on their goodwill tour, he and Uncle Bill would traditionally put on a double act during courses. It was supposed to replicate a complicated and very funny routine by American comedians Bud Abbot and Lou Costello about baseball players and the positions they played in. Charlie and dad always made a mess of it, but as it was Christmas, another tradition was that the guests pretended not to notice.

Brother John and I would be next to our father, and at the other end on the seat nearest the door would be Mother, managing the flow of food to the table with the help of Auntie Jill. Jill was not a real auntie, but had been taken in as an orphan by Grandfather and Grandma East. They had given her a roof over her head, and she worked countless hours in their pub. In those days, all pubs shut on Christmas Day, so Grandpa and Grandma would be dining with us.

Alongside them would be my mother's eldest sister Norah and her husband, and across from them my uncles Bill and Charlie and Charlie's wife Olive. Bill and Charlie were Mother's younger brothers, and, though they didn't look it, twins. Their mother had died giving them life, which may have been another reason their grandfather put his head in the gas oven. The motherless boys had been sent to Greenwich Naval School, and had served in and survived the War. It had been a near thing for Charlie, as he had been on the Atlantic convoys and shipwrecked twice. Bill was still on the MTB (Motor Torpedo Boat) *Wave*, and stayed with us when in port. Once a month, the captain would invite officers' families on board, and it was a huge treat for me to sit and gorge on a tin of sweet ship's biscuits and great chunks of the chocolate used to make the hot drink known as 'kye'.

As a Chief Petty Officer, Uncle Bill was also able to bring home the occasional treat. It was an old Naval tradition that the petty officer with the largest thumb would serve out the crews' daily tots of 'Pussers' rum*. When filling the measuring jug, he would keep his thumb in it and the leftovers would then be shared out amongst the petty-officers. I don't know how true the story was, but Uncle Bill would regularly arrive with a bottle of Pusser's best. This year, he and my dad were in mourning as Mother had found and used the whole bottle to give the Christmas cake added flavour. As my dad said ruefully, he and Bill would be eating a lot of cake this year.

'Pusser' was naval talk for the purser, the man on board responsible for stocking the ship before a voyage. In Nelson's navy he wasn't always a popular figure as some Pursers were known to order rotten food and supplies at a knock-down price and keep the savings.

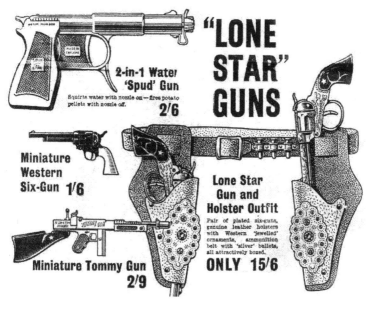

Nowadays, we chomp our way through ten million turkeys at Christmas.

The tradition of a turkey for Christmas began in Victorian times, but in the war they, like nearly everything else, were in short supply. Less than a decade before our 1953 gathering, a typical Christmas dinner would be carrot soup followed by rabbit with potato cakes. Pudding might be a delicious carrot fudge. No wonder we made the most of a post-War Christmas.

The gargantuan meal of 1953 ended with a Christmas pudding, boiled in muslin cloth and the size and shape of a football. Like the cake it was flavoured with pusser's rum, topped with a sprig of holly and set alight before being brought to table. Depending on household budgets, one or more silver sixpences or threepenny bits would be cooked in with the pudding, and it was the server's job to make sure the children found them.

The meal proper over, the adults would stay at table until able to walk, and be plied with drinks, nuts and dates and my favourite cheesy footballs and other snacks to help with digestion. The women would puff on posh cigarettes and the men would smoke cigars for probably the only time in the year. As I have said before, although commonplace today, the smell of a cigar still takes me back to a childhood Christmas.

Then, as three o'clock approached, in ten million homes the table would be cleared and tidied and glasses charged to make ready for a visit from our beloved monarch. People might leave the cinema early to avoid standing for the National Anthem, but to miss the Queen's Speech at Christmas would be unthinkable.

~

The ritual of the Monarch's Christmas Message was a tradition begun by George V in 1932. The 1953 Message was broadcast from Auckland in New Zealand at the start of a six-month tour of the Commonwealth by her Majesty and the Duke of Edinburgh. This is an extract which, I think gives a fair example of the tenor and tone:

"Some people have expressed the hope that my reign may mark a new Elizabethan age. Frankly I do not myself feel at all like my great Tudor forbear, who was blessed with neither husband nor children, who ruled as a despot and was never able to leave her native shores.

But there is at least one very significant resemblance between her age and mine. For her Kingdom, small though it may have been, and poor by comparison with her European neighbours, was yet great in spirit and well-endowed with men who were ready to encompass the earth.

Now, this great Commonwealth, of which I am so proud to be the Head, and of which that ancient Kingdom forms a part, though rich in material resources is richer still in the enterprise and courage of its peoples."

"I want to show that the Crown is not merely an abstract symbol of our unity but a personal and living bond between you and me."

With the dinner and Her Majesty's Christmas Message digested, it was time for the fun and games.

Across the nation, families would be playing the same parlour games. They would be the same games as the year before and the best part of a decade before that. Familiarity bred comfort rather than contempt in those post-war years. We had come through a period of death and destruction and possible subjugation by an evil Axis. Now we wanted things to get back to normal and stay there.

Physical games mostly involving the children would include musical chairs, hide and seek and pin-the-tail-on-the-donkey. Pass-the-parcel was a variation on musical chairs, with a many-layered parcel being passed around and the winner being the one who tore off the last sheet of wrapping to reveal and claim the prize. Another popular passing game would be two teams competing to be first to transfer a balloon between their legs. When the game was played by adults it was considered racy indeed.

Posher families played Charades; we played Forfeits and Consequences.

This old favourite involved Mother writing down a series of challenges on scraps of paper, with entrants choosing one from a hat. On the paper they would be instructed to undertake a task like Standing on One leg and Holding up Four, or Biting Four Inches off a Red-Hot Poker.

We all knew what was coming, but watched and waited in pleasant anticipation as Uncle Albert stood on one leg and held up a dining chair, or Auntie Norah took the poker and clamped her teeth shut a few safe inches away from the red-hot end.

A round of applause would follow the completion of a challenge, but deliberate failure would mean the loser paying the price in the form of a Consequence. For the men it might be a visit to the zoo to see a gorilla, when they were blindfolded and led to stand in front of a mirror.

For the ladies it might be having to put a finger in Nelson's empty eye socket. The socket would be the end of a peeled orange, and, although knowing exactly what was coming, the victim would squeal convincingly before her blindfold was removed.

It was all very childlike or even childish, but as I have said so often in preceding pages, we were all so easily pleased in those far-away days.

~

At the end of the day of excess, the guests would depart tipsily after much hugging and well-wishing, usually still wearing their paper hats. Taxis were a rare luxury, and one of the car-owners would usually ferry the guests home. In those pre-breathalyser days, the test for the owner being deemed fit to drive was whether he could stand and walk to the car unaided.

When our guests were gone, Mother, dad, John and I would sit together in comfortable silence by the front room fire. Dad would have a glass or two of Guinness and a large whisky, Mother a glass of port and John and I would have unlimited access to the Corona bottles while the chestnuts popped and split open on the coals.

This year I remember going out into the yard before bedtime, looking up at the night sky and thinking how perfect was my small, protected world. Every year we were reminded of the poor people around the world - and much closer to home - for whom Christmas would be just another cold, hungry and miserable day. I suppose I and other privileged children did give them a thought, but in those days charity began very much at home.

~

After the excitement and excesses of Christmas, New Year's Eve was no big deal for the children, but a valued excuse for the adults to party.

Families and friends would gather at home for drinks before it was time to take to the street for *Auld Lang Syne*. Doors would open and people spill out to link arms and sing lustily as ship's sirens sounded and whistles blew and the Guildhall clock chimed. Then would come an orgy of hand-shaking and back-slapping and kissing which I and the rest of the Castle Road Knights did their best to avoid.

The final ceremony was the first foot-in, a tradition my father had brought with him from Glasgow. The Hogmanay custom was that the first visitor to the house after midnight would be a tall, dark man, bearing a lump of coal to ensure the house would not go short in the coming year.

Being tall, dark and handsome, dad was always in demand, though barred by my mother from crossing any threshold where the lady of the house was young and pretty and single… or available.

~

Back at school after the Christmas holidays, we would compete to show off our presents in the playground. These were some of the most popular:

Blow football: A simple but entertaining game with the box as the pitch, a goal at each end, a ping-pong ball and two straws.

Space radio set: Plastic was now taking over from wood, tin and lead for toys, which was good news for parents of little boys who liked sucking on their collection of lead soldiers. This allegedly technological break-through enabled the users to talk to each other over a distance of, well, yards. In fact, the two handsets worked in exactly the same way as the good old favourite of using two tin cans with a length of string stretched between them*.

The Slinky: A magical spring which would walk down the stairs and oblige with all sorts of other tricks. I tried fixing two to the heels of my plimsolls so I could jump over high buildings like Spring-Heeled-Jack**, but it didn't work.

X-Ray Specs: In a time when advertising laws were much more relaxed, it was claimed this new invention would allow the wearer to see through solid walls and even women's clothing. Of course they didn't, but it was fun giving the girls a fright in the playground.

Seebackroscope: Sounded very scientific, but was actually a cardboard periscope as used by officers in the trenches in the Great War with the top mirror pointing behind the user.

Meccano: Every schoolboy's top-of-the-list present and the then equivalent of Lego. Kits went from very simple bolt-together strips of metal to complex and very expensive rigs complete with motors so you could build your own windmill, steam engine or sort-of working space ship.

Kaleidoscope: A bit girly for most boys, and was more or less a cardboard tube with a peep-hole at one end and assorted loose bits and pieces at the other. You shook it and looked at the pretty patterns.

3D Viewmaster: This was state-of-the-art technology, and looked like a small plastic binocular. At one end you slotted in two cardboard discs containing matching transparencies of exotic scenery and famous landmarks. When viewed, they sprung out of the frame at you and you could have been standing at the foot of the Eiffel

Tower. Younger readers might be surprised at how little it took to fill us with wonder at the latest marvels of technology.

Gyroscope: Another wonder of modern science. A metal wheel in a frame, it came complete with pull string and a model of the Eiffel Tower to balance it on. You set it going and it would balance almost anywhere.

Yo-Yo: It can be traced back thousands of years, but spinning a wheel on the end of a piece of string first became a craze in the 1920s, then had a revival every decade or so.

Magic Robot Quiz Game: This was a real technological advance in board games, although it was not much of a game. The box came with a small plastic robot holding a long pointer. You put him on a mirrored surface and aimed his pointer at a question, then moved the robot to a selection of answers. Miraculously, the robot would move round and point his stick to the right answer. We knew it was all done with magnets, but it was impressive until you got bored with it.

Airfix models: a wide range of models of ships, planes and cars in plastic parts which you glued together. The first aircraft was a Supermarine Spitfire Mk I, which came out in 1953.

Balsa-wood Plane kits: Putting together a model plane from balsa wood and tissue paper was an absorbing and delicate process. When assembled and painted with 'dope' to stiffen the paper, you hung it from your bedroom ceiling. Some models could actually fly with the addition of a propeller and a length of strong rubber attached to a wind-up propeller. I was far too impatient to go through the process, and usually broke my friends' working models when I over-wound the propeller and caused terminal implosion.

Jetex engines: Jetex 'engines' were little metal containers which you fixed to balsa wood models of planes or cars or boats. A pellet was placed in the container and a fuse attached. If you got it right, there was lots of hissing and smoke and your vehicle moved a few yards till the pellet burned itself out.

Another use for tin cans was to make what we liked to think of as stilts. A length of string was looped and each end passed through opposite sides of the circumference and knotted. The user would then step up on to the tins, and the trick would be to keep the string taut enough to prevent a malfunction and potentially painful tumble.

**Spring-heeled-Jack was an urban myth, first allegedly spotted in Victorian London and then across the country, including as a wraith in a cemetery in Portsmouth. He was the source of inspiration for a number of comic characters who used old bed springs to emulate his feats.*

1954

Fourteen years of rationing comes to an end as restrictions on the sale and purchase of meat and bacon are finally lifted. The first Wimpy Bar in the UK is opened in London. Lord Montague of Beaulieu and others are convicted of 'buggery and related charges', and the Wolfenden Committee is set up to investigate Homosexuality and Prostitution. 'The Grove Family', Britain's first TV soap opera is launched by the BBC, and the first episode of Hancock's Half Hour is aired. Roger Bannister becomes the first man to run a four-minute mile and Chris Chataway beats the world 5000 metres record by five seconds. The first two volumes in The Lord of the Rings series by JRR Tolkien are published, as is Ian Fleming's James Bond adventure, Live and Let Die. Britain agrees to end its occupancy of the Suez Canal. Popular recordings included 'Let Me Go Lover' by Joan Weber, 'Melancholy Baby' by Georgia Gibbs and 'Muskrat Ramble' by The Matys Brothers. Meanwhile, a little-known singer from America releases 'That's All Right Mama'. His fans know him as Elvis the Pelvis.

Times were still changing, and there were hints of the shape of things to come.

The last ration books had become redundant and, thanks to the televised Coronation, the number of TV licences had rocketed from 700,000 to 3.2 million. Despite dread forecasts that it would kill the art of conversation, divide the family and turn us into a nation of goggle-eyed morons, The Box was here to stay. Whether the dire predictions proved to have any substance depends on your personal point of view.

It was clear that we were heading for a very different future, but Britain was still a pretty grey, buttoned-up post-war sort of place. Teenagers had yet to be invented, and most boys of my brother's age went out at weekends in their school blazer, or grey flannels and a tweed jacket and dull tie just like their dads. James Dean, Teddy Boys and the cult of Youth were just around the corner, but we were still more attuned to pre-War morals and ways of acting and thinking.

National Service and short-back-and-sides haircuts were still in force, and a stiff upper lip in the face of adversity was the default attitude. Angst and stress were not words in common usage and nobody thought to tell us how hard-done-by we were. In fact, they constantly told us how lucky we were to live in modern Britain and to have survived the War. We children dimly understood the horrors and carnage that had gone before, but to us, bombsites were adventure playgrounds and nasty Nazis were sausage-eating, clod-hopping inhabitants of comic strips. As Prime Minister Harold MacMillan would be reminding us in a couple of years, we had indeed Never Had it so Good.

In the home, things were changing rapidly. By now, coming up for half the homes in Britain had bathrooms, though that meant that more than half did not. For us, 1954 was to be the Year of The Bathroom, though according to Mother it was installed mostly to attract a better class of lodger. Until and even after the dazzling white enamelled bath and rumbling geyser appeared, most working people maintained the view of one bath a week being quite sufficient. We washed every day at the kitchen sink, but mostly only the visible bits. I liked to sit and watch my dad make his morning ablutions in cold water, even on the coldest of days.

Stripped to the waist, he would soap his lean body carefully, sluice the lather away, then use a cupful of hot water from the kettle to shave.

I was particularly fascinated by the daily ritual, and longed for the time I'd be old enough to take it up. After using his new-fangled Rolls safety razor, he would turn the tap on full belt and stick his head beneath it. Having applied the 'tapolina' dressing, he would run a comb through his lustrous, wavy black hair and check in the mirror over the sink that he had got the centre parting straight. Then he would brush his teeth, turn, roguishly flex his muscles while giving me a big wink and smile. Sometimes I'd get a hug, and the smell of carbolic soap and Eucryl tooth powder stays with me. Even today, the memory of a cold, stand-up wash at the kitchen sink seems somehow more hygienic than lying prone in a tub-full of dirty water.

~

Regardless of the daily routine, Friday night was bath night for millions of Britons; for others it was Saturday evening, meaning you would be nice and clean for putting on your Sunday best.

After tea each Friday, dad would unhook the old zinc bath from the nail in the wall next to the outside toilet. In the scullery he would fill it with hot water from the boiler, then drag it into the kitchen and in front of the fireplace. In winter there would be a fire with towels warming above it, and the bath ceremony would be timed to coincide with popular radio programmes. I can see people in tin baths all over Britain enjoying *In Town Tonight*, when (as the slogan said) the mighty roar of London's traffic was stopped. This was done so bandleader Henry Hall could bring us music from the BBC light orchestra and a selection of visiting stars of stage, silver screen and radio.

Mother would of course not bathe with us, but make her own discreet arrangements at another time. The rule for order of immersion was cleanest in first and dirtiest in last. As John was becoming interested in girls he was usually the cleanest, while I was invariably last in line, even when dad was doing labouring work. I remember it as a jolly time of water pistols, thrown flannels and splashing and laughter which brought the inhabitants of the Mousey cupboard scurrying out to join in the fun if the coast was clear.

In those times, mice were a fact of life in almost every home. Most people kept a cat and also used mouse-traps, but the combination did no better than water pistols to keep the numbers down to an acceptable level. One of my jobs was to check and reset the traps, and I was always secretly pleased to find the bait gone and no tiny bodies trapped beneath the sprung wire.

~

After the zinc bath had been dragged back into the yard and emptied over the veg patch, we would get dressed and settle down for the evening. Dad would fill his pipe with Digger Shag, light it up and put his feet up on the mantlepiece to study form in the sports section of the Evening News. Having collected the wet towels and mopped the lino and replaced the rag rug in front of the fireplace, Mother would make supper. I'd be on the floor under my father's endless legs playing with a toy, while brother John would have retired to our room to practice combing his wet hair into a 'DA'. This was the hairstyle of choice for all aspirant Teddy Boys, and involved creating 'wings' of hair on either side of the head, meeting at the back in a fair approximation of a duck viewed from behind. Thus the DA or Duck's Arse, which was considered quite shocking and rebellious in those far-off days. There were no deodorants in those days, but it had been noted that John had, much to dad's amusement and my disgust, taken to the feminine habit of shaking perfumed talcum powder under his arms.

As a light supper of doorsteps of dripping toast and Bovril arrived, we would settle down to listen to the evening's offerings on the Light Programme.

It is difficult for anyone under pensionable age to understand the unifying power and popularity of BBC radio output in those days. It wasn't that the programmes were always entertaining or even particularly interesting; it was because it was a near-magical way of bringing other people, places and worlds into our homes. Although Christopher and Robin had their own vintage gramophone, not even the Fitzgeralds had a TV set. As they could easily have afforded one, I suspect that was by choice. In those days the middle classes mostly abhorred the idea of doing something so vulgar as watching television.

But for millions, the 'wireless' was a friend and companion and source of entertainment. During the day there was *Housewife's Choice* and *Music While You Work*. *Worker's Playtime* was piped into many factories, and in the evening it might be a play or a talk or *Semprini Serenade* or *Blackpool Night Out*, promising a 'galaxy' of stars.

At weekends, listeners were spoiled for choice, or so we thought then. Nowadays it is curious that the more tv channels on offer, the less we value what they show. As with television programmes in those days, listening choice was severely restricted, and somehow this meant we prized what we were given.

Among the most popular programmes were children's favourites on Saturday morning, and The Billy Cotton Band Show and the armed forces request programme on Sundays while the roast dinner was being prepared. As with cigars and Christmastime, when I hear *With a Song in my Heart* (the theme tune of *Two-Way Family Favourites*) I instantly recall the distinctive aroma of those long-gone Sunday lunches.

Everyone thinks that humour was funnier in their day, but I think it would be generally agreed that this was a golden era for radio comedy shows. Many have even stood the cruel test of time. There was the first-ever sitcom, *Life with the Lyons* and the utterly brilliant *Hancock's Half Hour*. Then there was *Educating Archie*, which defied logic as a radio show starring a ventriloquist and his dummy. *The Goon Show* was a new and very different weekly show, and it took me some time to get the anarchic humour. It was also an era of memorable radio dramas, and the most unmissable for me and millions of others was *Journey into Space*.

It followed the exploits of Jet Morgan and his colleagues Lemmy, Mitch and Doc amongst the stars, and was the last radio programme to outdo any television audience. It started my fascination for science fiction, and after each episode I was allowed to use the front room for my own space adventures.

I would arrange a bedspread over the table and lay a dining chair on its back on either side of my rocket-ship to act as booster engines. Another chair would be positioned under the table with the legs (actually ray guns) pointing forward and the seat removed to make the pilot's cockpit. Then I'd put on the old-World War II gasmask which was kept in the shed ('just in case' as my mother would say) and crawl under the bedspread to my cockpit and control centre. For some reason at this time I took to calling outer space 'canopy', which may have been because of the bedspread. Then it was countdown and blast-off and I'd journey to distant worlds and galaxies, take on and conquer aliens and perilous situations until bedtime called me back to Earth base. Even without or perhaps because of the lack of any virtual technology, it was all very real.

I vividly remember the almost overwhelming sense of excitement as I set out on my space adventures. I think that shows how, at any time in history, all a child needs to be entertained or even enthralled is his or her imagination.

~

In the days before we slumped on sofas watching television programmes about people slumped on sofas talking about television programmes, families had to entertain themselves.

A generation before, homes would have an upright piano in the parlour and each member of the family would be expected to have a 'turn'. Most commonly it would be a song, but there might be a stirring poem or comic recitation or poetry recital. After WWII, remnants of that tradition hung on, but musical evenings, recitals and games like Charades were mostly restricted to

Christmas or birthday parties. Otherwise and although individually occupied, the family would spend the evenings together in the same room.

Mother would invariably be knitting or darning. I read recently that society began to change when we stopped mending socks and just threw them away and that does seem to be a symptom if not a cause.

Dad might be re-soling shoes in the scullery, studying form in the sports section of the Portsmouth News or sorting out his football pools forecast. In wintertime I might be reading, drawing or creating coded top-secret messages for my gang with a John Bull printing set. Often I'd be making things from broken household items, often things that had been broken by me. I remember making a sonic ray gun from a terminally-ill bicycle pump and an old metal funnel, and a rocket launcher from a damaged length of guttering. More advanced projects in the shed or yard included a soapbox tank created from a badly holed zinc bath sitting upside down on a set of pram wheels.

In thousands of homes across Portsmouth, families like ours would be pleasantly occupied with hobbies and pastimes while listening to programmes like *Ray's a Laugh* or *Children's Favourites* with Uncle Mac on the Light Programme. Boys would be poring over their stamp or cigarette card collection, staging battles with toy soldiers or making tanks from a cotton reel, an elastic band and a lolly stick. Girls would be preparing for their futures by playing with dolls and miniature kitchens or making rugs with offcuts of wool and a crochet hook.

Another essential feminine leisure activity was making neat covers for schoolbooks out of brown wrapping paper. On the cover would be the owner's name and extended address:

This book belongs to Mary Smith
27 Olinda Street
Fratton
Portsmouth
Hampshire
England
Great Britain
The World
The Solar System
The Universe
The Galaxy

Meanwhile, titular heads of the households might be scraping out their pipes, practicing their party piece of playing the spoons, or making scale models of Stephenson's Rocket or even the *Titanic* out of matches in the shed. We read a lot in our house, and I can still remember the thrill of being swept away to another world by the adventures of Ralph Rover, Jack and Peterkin in *Coral Island*.

Nights were long and cold and money was always tight, but gathered together in front of the fire we felt snug, mostly contented and above all, safe.

~

The closing months of 1953 had been particularly mild, but made up for it as a new year got under way.

It was so cold I would ignore and hurry past the white-frosted bomb-dumps on my way to school, ready for the morning warm-up sessions in the playground.

Lined up in classes, we would follow instructions and pummel the back of the child in front. At the command, we would turn round and repeat the process. This was good if the person in front of you was someone you enjoyed bashing, but not so much fun if you were between two hefty boys or even some of the bigger girls.

The warming-up routine was necessary because the inside of the school was hardly warmer than the outside, and some of the poorer family's children had no decent winter clothing.

I think it is or can be true that hard times bring out the best and worst in people. In spite of their own tight budgets, there were many examples of compassion and pure kindness from ordinary working people. Good-hearted teachers would bring old coats and gloves and Balaclavas in and discreetly hand them over to the most deprived children. Parents would also help out in this way, but others were not so thoughtful or understanding and would visit their contempt for what they saw as shiftless and idle parents onto their children.

Like today, some pupils could be merciless with those weaker than themselves, and I remember coming upon a graphic example in Smith's Lane after school. A small, painfully thin boy in ragged shirt, shorts and boots with no socks was surrounded by a baying group of boys. When I pushed my way through, I saw that the child had suffered what we used to call an 'accident'. Perhaps caused by a combination of poor diet, stomach cramps or the icy cold, his bowels had given way and there was a slimy brown trail running down the inside of his legs. The spectators were mostly enjoying the entertainment, and it was reminiscent of an old engraving of a crowd at a bear baiting. I felt so angry and humiliated for the boy, I threw myself at the noisiest tormentor when he picked up a stone and threw it at the cowering figure. When he got over the shock, he turned on me and the crowd had a new source of entertainment.

It was my first proper fight, and taught me a couple of lessons. One was that being hit was painful, and another that once you start you have to keep on until you win - or lose. I was hurt and frightened, but the fear of losing and being mocked must have been greater than the fear of pain. Luckily for me, the fight was broken up by the blacksmith before I suffered too much damage. He was not a big man, but the sight of him charging out of his workshop wielding a pair of horseshoe tongs was enough to set us all on our heels. It also let the small boy with the soiled legs escape.

When I got home I expected Mother to be angry about my torn shirt, bloodied nose, and start of a black eye. But she had already heard what had happened from the mother of a schoolmate, and treated me with deep tenderness. Brother John was clearly impressed, and dad promised to show me how to award a Glasgow Kiss (head-butt) for next time, and sent me down the road to Tubby Bartholomew's tuck shop with a threepenny piece for a bag of sweets and bottle of pop.

At school the next day I seemed to have expanded my circle of friends, and some of the older boys made a point of acknowledging me. Even Mr Burns seemed to nod approvingly when our eyes met at Assembly. I probably imagined this general change of attitude, but I think the incident gave me a taste for using my fists in what seemed a good cause. This wasn't all altruism, but because I liked the idea of being a protector of the weak like my favourite comic book heroes.

As I was to learn the hard way, life is rarely like a comic book.

The term wore on, and I was still sitting at the back of the class trying to complete my drawing of the wounded knight.

Lessons went mostly over my head, except English and History, though my lack of interest or enthusiasm was down to me, not my teachers. I think I was too easily bored, always wanted to be somewhere else and doing something different rather than storing up information and qualifications for the future. Sadly, I never learned my lesson from missing out on all those lessons. After hundreds of mostly dead-end jobs and some modest success as a broadcaster and writer, I still want to be somewhere else and doing something else, no matter how pleasant the present may be.

Outside the classroom, I loved the rough and tumble of playground games and quite enjoyed getting involved in sports - or at least those in which being seriously overweight gave me an advantage. A good example was on sports day when I broke all records in the cricket-ball throwing competition by chucking it over the main building to land in a pile of horse poo in Smith's Lane.

I particularly liked cricket practice in the covered yard, where we used a wooden block to hold the stumps up. I remember we shared a battered bat and mismatched pads and gloves and had no box to protect our most sensitive area. We played with an old, out-of-shape but still very hard cricket ball, so I quickly learned to be best at defensive shots. I don't remember there being a school cricket team but that might be because I was not considered good enough to play in it.

There was a football team, and I joined because of the perks rather than any special interest in the game. Team members got special treatment, and time off lessons for what was laughingly called 'training' in the playground. As with milk and ink monitoring, I volunteered for and got the job of looking after the school kit. I figured this would be a cushdy post, and give me more time off lessons while pretending to count shinpads and check that the school football was fully inflated. I got the job, but my cunning scheme turned out to be an own goal. This was because part of my duties was to keep clean and maintain all the pairs of school-owned boots. In those days, few parents could afford a pair of soccer boots or strip for their son, so a collection of shirts, shorts and boots were kept in the sports cupboard. It was a first-come-first-served arrangement, so the biggest and fleetest boys got first choice. This wasn't a problem with the kit as real footballers wore the longest and baggiest of shorts and ours came in a one-size-fits-all selection. It was, though, a problem with the boots. If they were too big, you risked leaving them behind on a muddy pitch. If they were too tight, you would only be able to hobble rather than run after the ball. Whatever their size or age, football boots were not the feather-light and supple creations of today. In fact, they were more like the footwear of deep-sea divers. Unless regularly pummelled and massaged and treated with a waxy substance known as dubbin, they would become totally rigid. Luckily for me, also being the ink and milk monitor I was able to bribe or bully classmates to do the dirty work.

On the field of play and having no interest or a shred of talent and being fat and slow on my feet, I was a natural for goalie. I spent my brief career lounging against a goalpost while watching the other twenty-one players chasing around the pitch, mostly after the ball but often after each other.

State-of-the-art soccer strip circa 1954

For most people born in Britain more recently than sixty years ago, a world without constant and freely available hot running water must be almost unimaginable.

If you are a modern woman who is devastated when the washing machine blows a fuse, spare a thought for what every housewife had to do to keep the family's clothes clean.

In itself, the sheer slog of washing day explains why mothers got so angry when their sons came home looking like they had been mudlarking down at the Hard. Keeping the family laundry respectably clean was a constant, thankless and physically demanding job. But it had to be done, and it was always done on a Monday.

A small but important mystery I never solved is why the day for the weekly wash was so inviolable. Monday was washday, and that was it, come rain or shine or even snow.

Like every other house in the road and probably in the city, we had a scullery, which was no more than a small lean-to room stuck on the back of the house. It would invariably have a red painted stone floor, whitewashed walls and very small windows to keep the heat from escaping. There would be a connecting door to the kitchen/living room, and another would lead to the back yard and the outside toilet and shed. As well as garden tools, old gas masks and prams with missing wheels (pinched for our soapbox racers) and the odd rat, the shed might be home to a couple of chickens who would spend the day scratching around on a tiny veg patch.

Whatever the weather, the scullery always smelled dank and sourly damp. This would be particularly so on a Monday washday, but at all other times because of the rising and penetrating damp, condensation and rain finding its way through the roof.

In one corner would be what we called a Butler or Belfast sink and usually in the middle of the floor would stand a waist-high boiler called a 'copper'. It would have a wooden lid and be surrounded by bricks or plaster. In previous generations the water would have been heated by a coal or wood fire; Mother and her generation mostly had the luxury of a gas supply.

My memories of washday are a bit foggy as I'd be at school, or out and about during holidays. Occasionally I'd be around to watch the ceremony, or help if I was bored or short of pocket money.

While the water in the copper was heating, the dolly and its tub would be lugged in from the shed, or the cupboard where the dirty laundry was stored during the week. They varied, but our dolly tub was about the height and shape of a small-ish dustbin. With it came a strange device also made from wood, which was like a low, three-legged milking stool with a shaft attached and topped with a T-shaped handle. This giant agitator was the 'dolly' and was said to have got its name because of a vague resemblance to a doll.

Next, the dirty washing would be sorted out into whites and colours before going into the boiler.

In our house, the copper was used for dirty clothes that needed a boil, while those less soiled went straight into the dolly tub. Smaller items would be done by hand in the sink. This would include shirts needing their collars and cuffs scrubbed. In our family, the rule was one shirt on and the other 'in the wash'. This meant making a shirt last for the best part of a week, with just the collars and cuffs done as a temporary measure till washday. If any items needed extra attention, there was always the washboard, a sheet of corrugated zinc with a wooden frame. I don't remember my mother using one, but they came to prominent attention as instruments in the skiffle music craze of the 50's.

I have a vague memory of slivers of soap being shaved into the water in the copper and that temperature was vital. Too cold and the stains would stay in; too hot and some items would shrink.

As steam rose and condensation ran down the walls, it would be time to transfer the suitable items to the dolly tub. Twisting and turning and pounding with the dolly was a demanding task, especially in the steamy heat. That's why professional washerwomen were known for their big arms and sometimes their formidable punching power.

Now it was time for rinsing, which also took time and effort. At this stage the contents of what was confusingly known as a Reckitt's Blue Bag could be added to make whites, as the advert went, even whiter.

Finally and several hours later, the washing was ready for the line. In the case of rain, it would all be draped around the scullery and kitchen to dry.

It was a demanding way to start the week for millions of housewives, and had to be fitted in with all the other tasks. However hard the day had been, dinner would have to be on the table when the breadwinner's bike was pushed into the passageway.

Life for the working man could be dirty, demanding, demeaning and even dangerous, but at least he could take his ease when he shut the front door on the world. His wife would be at it from dawn to dusk and beyond, and there was never a truer observation than that a woman's work was never done.

~

When you think about the sheer physicality of their daily workload, it's not much of a surprise that the daily calorie requirements by women in the Fifties was considerably more than today. Without paying for gym memberships or dieting aids, the average housewife was slimmer and healthier than many women today. Before the days of labour-saving household appliances, they got their energy from a healthy diet of dripping toast and suet puddings, and burned off the calories by heavy household chores, lugging heavy shopping bags and children on foot or by bike. Of course there were overweight women then, but not in the numbers we see today.

It might not be feasible nowadays, but that was how the division of labour worked in millions of households in the 1950s. As I've said before, the norm was that dads would go out to work and bring home the bacon; mothers would keep the home fires burning, the family fed and the house clean. It may seem an unfair distribution of labour from a modern perspective, but as I have also said before, in those time we knew no better.

~

As mentioned earlier, there were some tasks the man of the house would be expected to take responsibility for. A good example was repairing the family footwear.

Nowadays shoes are so cheap they're given to a charity shop or thrown away when the owner gets fed up with them. Some find their way to far-away places where shoes are a luxury. In modern Britain, some women have so many pairs of shoes and fashion boots that they risk a nervous breakdown while agonising over which ones to wear. Some women have whole rooms set aside for their footwear and handbag collection, and I know couples who have moved to a bigger house to accommodate a variety and number of shoes and boots which would outdo a high street branch of Shoes R Us.

In the 1950s, some of the poorest people had literally nothing to put on their feet. Most working families might have a pair of shoes for everyday use and a pair for

Sunday best. This was because shoes were very expensive and built to last. Some would outlast the wearers. When times were hard, the leather soles would get ever thinner. The condition and thickness of the soles were a usually reliable indicator of the wearer's financial situation. That's where the expression of 'being on your uppers' came from. It was also a common joke that some people could tell the value of a coin they had stepped on when their soles were at the point of collapse. There were cobbler's shops which specialised in re-soling shoes, but most working-class homes preferred to save money by doing-it-themselves.

The basic item was a cobbler's last, which was a metal device in the shape of a foot on which the shoe under repair could be placed. The repairer would also need a sharp knife, a hammer and a tin of tacks.

The leather for the new sole came in sheets and I loved the tangy smell. Making it fit on to a pair of shoes required a degree of skill and had a positive result, and was a job my dad liked doing. I remember watching in admiration as he sat cross-legged on the kitchen floor with a mouthful of tacks, concentrating on and taking pride in making a pair of shoes wearable for years to come.

~

With dad sent off to work and John and I at school, Mother would get down to the real work of the day.

As Monday was marked down for washday, there would be days set aside for other weekly jobs like window cleaning, carpet beating and baking. Making the beds, 'airing' the house, cleaning, shopping, cooking and repairs on clothing, furniture and the house itself happened every day.

Nowadays, people seem to want their homes to be kept clean to the standard of a hospital operating theatre.

Some modern kitchens and bathrooms I've seen *look* like operating theatres. Back then and perhaps because of the lack of household aids, people learned to live with a little grime. In fact, rather than cause horror, exposure to bugs, dust and sometimes elderly food was thought to build up a healthy resistance to disease. For many families, the eat-by-date on any item of foodstuff would be based on smell rather than appearance. As a popular saying had it, if a meat pie didn't move when you approached it, it was clearly edible.

Credit Chrissy Ayling Bennett

Going to the Flicks

Despite the attentions of the Luftwaffe there was no shortage of picture palaces in Portsmouth in the mid-Fifties. Some had started life as theatres, some were purpose-built. As society's needs and wants changed, these often-magnificent buildings were condemned to become bowling alleys or bingo halls or supermarkets. But in their heyday, a weekly visit to the flicks was a real treat.

The 1951 Kellys Directory names eighteen what they called Cinematograph theatres in the city. Like Pompey pubs, they ranged from the sumptuous and often completely over-the-top 'picture palaces' to what we quite accurately called flea pits or bug hutches. To get a picture of how popular going to the flicks was then, it's recorded that in 1954 there were more than 1.6 billion visits to British cinemas. Although the cinema-going 'experience' has had a revival in recent years, the total visits for last year were a measly 1.7 million.

Like TV nowadays, cinemas played a major part in our lives, and there was a real range in architectural style and condition. The Odeon in Highland Road had been built in the 1930s and was a wonderful example of late art-deco. Where the imposing building stood is now a small housing estate, while the magnificent, soaring tower of its twin in North End looks down sadly at the shops which now trade in its interior. The Gaumont at Bradford Road junction was approached up an impressive set of steps and inside was the size of an aircraft hangar. It's now a mosque, while the Troxy in Fratton Road ended its days as a cut-price shoe store.

Nowadays, nearly every home has a gateway to escapism. You can watch any of a hundred movies, play golf with Tiger Woods or kill an army of Zombies before teatime. In those days, it was a big deal to go to the flicks, and people actually dressed up for the occasion. The first feature film I remember seeing at the Southsea Odeon was *20,000 leagues Beneath the Sea*. It came out in 1954, was in glorious, almost breath-taking colour and starred James Mason as the enigmatic Captain Nemo. Compared to what had gone before in terms of picture quality and special effects, it was a real blockbuster.

But cinemas then offered more than a place to see a movie. Like thousands of Portsmouth children, I was a regular visitor to the Saturday Morning Picture Clubs. Members of the Odeon Club had their own badge and song. It was sixpence to get in but free if you were a Monitor - or what we called the Hitler Youth. They were naturally bossy older children (mostly girls it has to be said) who strutted around swinging their torches and wearing armbands and a stern expression. Their job was to patrol the aisles and stop us throwing orange peel and empty ice cream tubs around and otherwise generally enjoying ourselves.

The entertainment would be a series of cartoons like Tom and Jerry and Popeye which always showed the hero (Jerry the mouse or Popeye the spinach-loving sailor man) defeating and inflicting very painful retribution on the villain (Tom the cat and Bluto).

The entertainment would finish with a dramatic 'cliff-hanger' serial, ending as rising water, moving walls and sharpened stakes (and sometimes all three) imperilled our hero and the damsel he was rescuing. Would they escape? Of course they would, or that would be the end of him and the series. It was all very predictable, but greedy for visual entertainment we had learned to suspend our disbelief and thrill to the action as Flash Gordon took on Ming the Merciless, and Gene Autry got his guitar out after polishing off at least a dozen whooping redskins or men in black hats. Naturally, as we spilled out into daylight and made our way home, we all recreated the adventures of our heroes. For some reason, I was always cast as the villain.

~

As well as the films each Saturday morning, there would be regular events on-stage in the intervals. A troupe of earnest girls would show us how to hula-hoop, or a small boy would play the accordion very badly. An occasional star visitor was Art Pickles, the world yo-yo champion. Or at least, champion of those parts of the world that played with yo-yos. He would arrive on stage and impress us with manoeuvres like Walking the Dog and Looping the Loop. I remember there was a competition to win a bicycle, but I was knocked out in the first round after the string broke and my yo-yo disappeared into the darkness beyond the footlights.

~

Whether or not we could afford the entry fee, 'copping in' or 'bunking in' to the flicks was a challenge we couldn't resist. Cinemas were graded for difficulty of entry, and one criterion was the nearness of the emergency exit to the Gents toilets. At the easy places, we would club together pay for one ticket. Our scout would be shown to his seat by a torch-bearing (and often suspicious) usherette. He would wait for the coast to be clear, then open the emergency exit doors. We would sneak into the toilets and innocently emerge at intervals, dispersing ourselves around the auditorium. If the usherette had reported her suspicions, our inside man might be kept under observation. If the manager wanted to join in the fun, he would set a watch on the door to the toilets and grab each of us as we emerged, much in the manner of escaping prisoners being captured in *Stalag17* or *The Wooden Horse*. We would then be guided by the ear or the scruff of the neck to the entrance and deposited on the pavement. I know some of the managers enjoyed the game and the police were never called in or our parents told. It was instant and painful justice, but just part of the game, and back then we hadn't been told how a clip round the ear could scar us mentally for life.

~

Another opportunity for a lark came when a cinema had a doorman or what was grandly called a commissionaire. Often ex-servicemen, they would be dressed up like Ruritanian generals with yards of ornate gold braid and tassels, and shoulder epaulettes the size of scrubbing brushes. Ironically, the more down-at-heel the cinema the more likely it was to have a commissionaire done up to the nines.

A good example was the Gaiety in Albert Road, a once-impressive building but increasingly decrepit as it headed towards its final incarnation as a supermarket. The commissionaire was an elderly (to us) man with a toothbrush moustache and a remarkable squint, enlarged by much-repaired bottle-bottom spectacles. The moustache sat beneath a pointy, red-tipped nose, which dripped incessantly on cold days. His uniform was worn and faded and a couple of sizes too big. The scrubbing brush epaulettes would hang out over his narrow shoulders and his hat would sit on his prominent ears and looked as if it would remain still if he turned his head too quickly.

Inevitably we called him Hitler, but not just because of his moustache. To us, anyone in authority could qualify. A caretaker or overzealous train or bus ticket inspector would be *Heil Hitler-ed* and given a stiff-armed salute from a safe distance.

With the emergency exit usually chained and locked, The Gaiety was impregnable. This made Old Hitler a natural target. When we could afford the price of a ticket it would make him grit and grind his false teeth to have to let us in and, worse, to have to open the door.

When we were broke or the film was of no interest, we'd taunt him from the pavement, goose-stepping in front of the steps and running off when he clattered down them. We knew he couldn't desert his post, so would give him some more stick, usually imitating his stiff-legged limp. For all we knew, he could have spent the war fighting the Nazis and been wounded in action. But small boys then - as now - could be cruel. We adored mythical comic book wartime heroes, but made no connection with real men who had fought for our freedom in two World Wars. It wasn't unusual then to see a man with an empty trouser leg swinging his way down the road on crutches, an empty jacket sleeve tucked into a pocket or a sometimes horrifically scarred face. Our world lacked today's sensitivity and compassion, and people with disabilities were regularly referred to as cripples. We would point out and follow interesting cases, and stare or even laugh as our victim struggled to get on a bus, open a door or just make his way down the street.

It was the same with all disabilities, however they had come about. One object of constant fascination was a man who sold papers in the city centre. He had some form of cancer which took the form of a horrendous scabby growth distorting his face and climbing like a ghastly stalagmite from his lower lip. It was said that he had become infected by his habit of putting copper coins in his mouth while making change. However it came about and however much he must have suffered, to our shame we saw him, like a deformed character in a comic book, as no more than a regular source of fascinated horror. Or worse, amusement.

~

Evidence of the popularity of the cinema in the Fifties was the size of the queues.

If it was a movie with a big-name star, you would need to arrive hours before the start to be sure of getting in. The queue at the Odeon in Southsea would often stretch along the frontage and round the corner into the car park. People would shuffle anxiously towards the box office, hoping to get there before the commissionaire put the rope barrier and *House Full* sign up. If you were lucky, you might be able to squeeze in to stand at the back. I don't know what the health and safety rules were then, but the Standing Room Only limitation on numbers seemed very elastic.

Once inside and if the lights had already dimmed, you would be shown to a seat by a torch-bearing usherette. The usual programme would include the main movie and what was known as a 'B' picture. These were made on a very tight budget and often badly written, filmed and acted. Some would be dire indeed.

In the same way as modern budget airline flights, where you sat and who with was an important factor. Unpopular neighbours were noisy courting couples, coughers or sniffers and noisy kids like us. A really fat person next to you would spill over on to your seat, and worst of all would be a tall man or a woman with a big hat in your line of vision. Behind might be a small child amusing himself by kicking the back of your seat or wailing for attention every five minutes. Smoking was the norm so no cause for complaint, but if you had a group of sailors around you there could be a literal smokescreen between you and the movie.

These were everyday hazards for adults, but there were occasionally more frightening ones for children. In those days, darkened cinemas were favoured hunting grounds for male predators. They would seek out a lone child to sit beside and, as we used to say, interfere with. It might start with an offer of a bag of sweets or a comment about the film. Sometimes, nothing was said before a hand stretched out and fondled a knee and then moved upwards.

It happened to me once, and I did nothing but sit rigid with fear and embarrassment till the lights came up and I could escape. I didn't report the incident to the manager or tell my parents or especially my mates. As I have said so often, things were very different then.

~

Patrons preferred different areas of the cinema for different reasons. A major consideration would be price. In the reverse of the theatre, the cheapest seats would be in the front rows because of the distorted images and risk of a stiff neck. The most expensive seats would be furthest away from the screen and up in the balcony.

Courting couples would usually be concerned more with location than with price and aim for the back row downstairs. The floor would slope upwards with a partition behind the back row and they could get down to business. On a cold winter's night and without a car, it was worth the admission fee to have somewhere warm and dark to snog. I know some couples went to the same film several times without seeing more than a few moments of the action on screen. It was generally pretty innocent stuff and no more than kissing, though some exploration of the upper body might be permitted. Usually, as they said, over the bra, and sometimes if the boy got really lucky, beneath it.

Part of the entertainment for us kids was spying on the couples, particularly if the B film wasn't worth watching. Some kids would give a running commentary on the clinches; others in the same row would find an excuse to constantly leave their seats so the couple would have to disentangle and stand up. Really pushy kids would charge a fee for them to go away and annoy another couple.

Upstairs in the gallery you got the best view of the screen and the front row was the perfect location. For the adults it meant an uninterrupted view of the screen; for us kids it was a perfect launching pad for paper darts, orange peel and empty drinks and ice cream containers.

Probably the best way to cause havoc was with a stink bomb. What were called 'pranks' were popular, and always involved upsetting or hurting innocent victims. The specialist novelty or joke shops were filled with plastic dog turds, farting cushions and itching powder. The squirting lapel flower was dated even then, but stink bombs were always popular with children. They were small, glass ampoules which let off a viciously rank smell of rotten eggs when broken. A favourite trick in the cinema was to sidle up the aisle, pretend to drop something and then place a stink bomb next to the victim. Your accomplice would then walk past and step on it. Another wheeze was to visit the toilet during the intermission and throw a bomb into an occupied cubicle. We would then run out, dramatically holding our noses and wait to point out the alleged culprit as he emerged to face the queue.

Apart from artificially-created pongs, the average cinema would be quite ripe in atmosphere, especially after rain. People had far fewer clothes and wore them for much longer in between washing. There was also no such thing as deodorant in common use. 'Perfumed' talcum powder and cheap scent would add to rather than mask the mix of smelly clothes and unwashed bodies.

Then there would be the pervasive aroma of stale cigarette and pipe smoke and even bowls of pease pudding or delicacies like pig's trotters or pickled onions to enjoy while watching the film.

I can't remember people or places being particularly smelly, but I suppose that was because, like not noticing the odour of garlic on other people's breath when you have eaten some, we were all very much in the same boat.

~

I don't suppose many people would stay on to watch a film again nowadays, but in those times it was quite normal. People came and went all the time and if you missed the start of the feature film it was only natural that you would wait till it came round again.

In fact, the only time the audience acted in unison would be just before the playing of the National Anthem. This happened at the end of each performance as the lights came up, and there would always be a rush to make it to the exit before the music began. Otherwise, you had no choice but to stand stock still with your hands down by your side as the opening bars of *God Save The Queen* struck up. It was not that we were unpatriotic, but stealing a march meant you avoided getting stuck in the throng and even worse, being at the back of a very long queue when the bus arrived.

Certificates of 'suitability for viewing' were granted by the British Board of Film Classification from 1912. By the Fifties, a 'U' (for 'Universal') certificate meant there was no age restriction. 'A' was for Adult Viewing, though curiously a child over 11 would be admitted. Anyone under 11 had to be accompanied by a parent or guardian. Any child could be admitted if accompanied by someone over 18, which is why we spent so much time hanging round cinema entrances to ask lone sailors to take us in. For the most horrific or sexuality explicit films there was the X rating. Only those over 16 were allowed in to see what most modern viewers would think was very tame stuff.

Cinematograph Theatres listed in 1951 Kelly's Directory of Portsmouth

(From- **Portsmouth-A Tale of One City**.)

Apollo Cinema, 42 Albert Rd
Carlton Cinema, High St Cosham
Classic Cinema, 151 Commercial Rd
Essoldo Cinema, 223 Kingston Rd
Forum Cinema, Stamshaw Rd
Gaiety Cinema, Albert Rd
Gaumont Cinema, Bradford Junction, Bradford Rd
New Queens Cinema, 10 & 12 Queen St
Odeon Theatres Limited: North End, High St, Cosham and Festing Rd, Southsea
Palace, 34 & 36 Commercial Rd
Regal Cinema, Eastney Rd, Eastney
Regent Theatre, 59 London Rd, North End
Rex Cinema, Fratton Rd
Savoy Cinema, Commercial Rd Landport
Shaftesbury Cinema, 140 & 142 Kingston Rd
Tivoli Cinema, 117 Copnor Rd
Troxy Cinema, Fratton Rd
Victoria Cinema, Commercial Rd

'We come along on Saturday morning, greeting everybody with a smile; we come along on Saturday morning knowing things are well worthwhile.'

(The official song of members of the Odeon Saturday Morning Picture Club, who even had their own badge.
The Gaumont also had its own club and some kids belonged to both. The postman would deliver a card on your birthday and a special invitation from Uncle Ray to come along for free with a friend.)

The ABC Minors' song

(To the sound of a band playing the marching music 'Blaze Away'.)

'We are the boys and girls well known as
Minors of the ABC
And every Saturday all line up
To see the films we like, and shout aloud with glee
We like to laugh and have a singsong
Such a happy crowd are we.
We're all pals together.
We're minors of the A-B-C!'

Sweet Life

Nowadays the demon sugar lies in wait everywhere, and children are a prime target. There are acres of sweets on display in shops and supermarkets and in TV ads. They are even lined up at child height at checkouts. Together with oceans of fizzy drinks and sugary foods and being chauffeured to school and spending most of their leisure time slumped in front of a screen, it's a surprise that more children are not the shape of a giant gob-stopper.

In the immediate post war years, we were not at much risk of overdosing on sugary treats.

Sweet rationing was in force up to 1953, and anyway there just wasn't the money about to lash out on sweets and snacks. Most children also spent almost every available moment outdoors. We were forever on the move playing street games, riding imaginary horses or walking what would seem enormous distances to many youngsters today. It's an irony that kids today do so little exercise, yet dress like athletes in track suits and trainers while they fight their virtual battles.

~

In the 1950s, a visit to a sweet shop was always a treat. For the children of poorer families, it could be a very rare treat. Despite a recent revival, shops selling nothing but sweets are very thin on the ground nowadays. In the Fifties they popped up everywhere and in some strange locations. All were different and had their own character and characters behind the counter. The posh ones would announce themselves as 'confectioners', while the most basic were often operated from someone's front room.

Within a mile of Castle Road there were dozens of sweet shops, and a classic was Ma Parkers. It seemed to be of another era even then. It was set in an early Victorian terraced house on the corner of a narrow alley, and customers went up three worn steps into the permanently cool and gloomy interior. I can remember the lines of boxes on the counter and jars on the back shelves, and the agony of indecision about what you would spend your few pence on. Would it be a gobstopper, some tiger or monkey nuts, a liquorice stick or a couple of ha'penny chews? On a hot day you might choose a ha'penny or penny Vantas. This was a wondrous device which looked like a crystal ball, fixed to the counter and filled with water. When you had chosen from a range of flavours, the syrup would be squirted into a paper cup which would then be topped up with fizzy water from the crystal ball. It would be wrong to say I remembered anything about the proprietor, and I suspect that was because I was much more interested in the sweets than the owner. In my mind's eye, though, she was always swathed in voluminous black clothing, had a little pill-box bonnet pinned to her grey hair and could have been the role model for Old Mother Kelly.

~

A regular stop on my way to school was a sweet shop in the front room of a tiny worker's cottage in Green Road. In those days, many people traded officially or discreetly from their homes to earn some extra money. At this one there was no name above the door, but it was open for business during school hours. A home-made counter with a rusty set of scales on it spanned the passageway, and lining a single shelf beneath the gas and electricity meters would be a sparse collection of jars and boxes. There was not much to choose from, but I was intrigued by the idea of having a sweet shop in your own home. I remember the proprietor as a tall, thin, mournful-looking man with long, grimy and skinny fingers. He never acknowledged my presence, and no words were exchanged beyond my making my order. I would point at a jar of lemon drops or chocolate bon-bons or sweet hearts and watch as he went through his routine like a stage magician performing a sleight-of-hand trick. He would reach down for a jar, unscrew the lid and always seemed to shake exactly the right weight into the scales.

Next would come the *piece de resistance*. There would be a stack of old newspapers on the counter, and he would carelessly tear off a page and fashion it into a cone in seconds. The sweets would be tipped inside and the top sealed with a deft twist of the fingers. I'd then be on my way and he would return to his seat in the passageway, looking gloomily out into the street as if wondering what he had done to end up there.

~

Another popular sweet shop was in Somers Road, opposite Cottage Grove school and next door to an establishment which sold animal feed - and in particular horse meat. The joints would be hung outside, some dripping blood and all painted green to show they were not for human consumption. Knowing the poverty levels in the area, I don't think it was only pets who would get to know the taste of horse meat.

The tuck shop next door was run by an affable one-legged man, who had an admirable if misplaced belief in the honesty of children.

In those days, few things were disposable and there would be a deposit charged on most soft drinks bottles.

When empty, you returned your bottle to the shop and got a penny reward.

The owner of our tuck shop would leave the crates of empty bottles stacked outside the front. This was too much of a temptation for some of us, and we would nick a bottle from a crate and take it in and claim the deposit. He was a very nice man and I still feel guilty about the deception, but it is too late to say sorry. At the time we eased our consciences by buying a packet of broken crisps* with the penny while falsely reasoning that Mr Peg-Leg was getting his money back.

A more ambitious scam was perpetrated by my mate Tinker Jackson at shops which ran regular promotions for their home-made ice lollies. If you found the name of the shop on the stick, you could show it to the owner and claim a free lolly. Tinker had an accomplice with a John Bull printing kit, and would stamp and sell branded sticks for half the price of a lolly. The scheme collapsed when the shops realised they were giving away more lollies than they sold. So Tinker had had to close down the operation and find another lucrative scam.

*I heard only recently that Tony's broken crisps were distributed by two brothers who ran a cleaning company. The story goes that the local Smith's Crisps factory was a customer, and was where the broken and therefore officially unusable crisps came from. I remember that they were very salty and oily, and, as my informant's dad used to say, one packet of Tony's was worth twenty of Smith's...

~

According to a recent nationwide survey, the average weekly pocket money for adolescent children is around £6. Converted backwards to the mid-1950s, that would be a whopping five shillings (twenty-five pence). In our day, that princely sum would have allowed an orgy of sweet cigarettes, ha'penny chews, sherbet dabs, ice lollies and even a Mars bar every day.

According to a survey of Portmuthians of my vintage, there was no average in the 1950s, and a regular allowance was rare. Some children got no cash but were treated to sweets and comics once a week. Others were given film and bus money, and bought sweets by walking everywhere and bunking into the cinema.

Many did chores and errands for spending money. One lady recalled following a delivery horse and cart to collect manure for her dad's vegetable plot and earning a small fee per bucketload. Another remembered collecting newspapers and rags to sell to the salvage yard in Blackfriars Road. Some children of poor families like the O'Kelly's got no pocket money and no treats. They had to live on their wits and get up to no good if they wanted a bag of sweets or bottle of pop. Some with indulgent parents like mine got comics and sweets and pop paid for. As well as inventing scams, some of my more entrepreneurial schoolmates like George Langton and Tinker Jackson ran micro-businesses, selling rather than swapping items.

However much disposable income you had, visiting a sweet shop clutching a few coppers was a serious business. Would it be four blackjack chews for a penny, a packet of fake cigarettes or should you blow fourpence on a single Mars bar? Even in my privileged position I can't remember eating a Mars bar in one go, and it was usually cut into slices to eke out the pleasure or share with mates. Bagged (loose) sweets were sold generally in two-ounce (56g) portions. If you were really cash-rich you might go for a whole quarter pound. In the posher shops you would get an unused paper bag torn from a string hanging on a nail. Otherwise it would be the torn-off piece of newspaper, adroitly formed into a cone. Fish and chips were also sold in newspaper wrapping, hence the expression that today's news was tomorrow's fish and chip paper.

Despite the blame heaped on we baby-boomers' collective heads, we were all recyclers then. Not by choice, but by necessity.

The list of sweets popular in the 50s shows a liking for both sweet and sour tastes. Here's a selection, some of which are still going. My thanks as ever to the members of Memories of Bygone Portsmouth for their pocket money and sweet recollections:

Acid Drops
Aniseed Balls
Banana Splits
Barley Sugar Twists
Blackjack chews
Chocolate Drops
Chewits
Coconut Ice
Dolly Mixtures
Flying Saucers
Fruit Salad chews
Fry's Peppermint Cream Bars
Gobstoppers (changed colours as they shrank)

Humbugs
Jelly Babies
Liquorice Sticks (roots) and Pipes
Liquorice Reels (with a sweet stuck in the centre)
Love Hearts (had a message of endearment)
Milk Chews
Pineapple Cubes
Refreshers
Scented Cashews
Sherbet Dips
Sherbet Lemons
Spangles
Sweet Violets
Swizzle sticks (to dip into sherbet)
Sugar bon-bons (toffees covered in icing sugar)
Terry's Neapolitans
Tiger Nuts
Toffee Brittle
Wagon Wheels

A recent governmental report said that nine out of ten hospital extractions of children's teeth were because of decay caused by sugary food and drinks.

Thanks to sugar rationing and lack of funds, it was neglect rather than sugar that did for the teeth of many children in the 1950s. A memory that stays with me is the visit of the Schools Dentist. I remember ours as a huge ogre-like man with dirty fingernails. He had huge hands and used to shove a thumb in each corner of your mouth to expose your teeth. Then he would lean close and peer into your mouth, grunt and then dismiss you from the chair. Ironically, I remember he had very bad breath and big, discoloured tombstone teeth. He also sprayed a lot of saliva in your face while doing the close-up inspection.

I'm told that there were also regular visits from the Nit Nurse, but either I was away on the days she called or our encounters are locked away in the Tomb of Forgotten Memories. I seem to remember Mother examining my scalp every time I had been playing with any member of the O'Kelly clan, and on one occasion being doused with what smelled and looked like pink paraffin.

At school I was still doing the absolute minimum to get by and had learned to give the impression I was paying attention when I was actually taking on and thwarting German secret agents or brain-sucking aliens. A born sycophant, I found it a doddle to keep on the right side of the teaching staff, but I and my gang always seemed to be on the wrong side of Jack Frost.

In those days, every school had a caretaker, and they were not generally known for their liberal views or tolerance, especially if it involved small boys and any threat to the physical and moral structure of their school.

'Jack' Frost remains clearer in my memory than any of the teachers, and I can see his red-cheeked, angular, frowning face, bushy eyebrows, gimlet-sharp eyes and slicked-back silver hair in vivid detail. I don't know what he did in the War, but if he frightened the Germans as much as he frightened us, I reckon Victory in Europe could have come a lot sooner.

Of medium height and spare build and always in a bib-and-brace overall held in place at the waist with a wide leather belt and heavy ex-army boots, Mr Frost lived in a little cottage near the main gates. This was where he liked to stand guard when the school day began and ended. I don't think he was a bad man; just of his time. He was a disciplinarian and always on the lookout for the slightest breach of the rules or his idea of how we should conduct ourselves while on the premises. Although he would have got away with it in those days, I never saw him actually hit a child. He didn't need to, as his presence and expression was enough to keep us in order as we came and went. I don't remember him as a vindictive man; it was just that he regarded the school and every part of it as his responsibility, and he took his responsibilities seriously. The only time I remember him smiling was when the whole lower school was paraded in the rain when someone left a bad mess in the toilets. We were told we would have to stay there until the culprit owned up, and we did for more than an hour.

Modern-day educationalists would probably go into trauma to learn what went on in Cottage Grove as normal disciplinary practice, and corporal and even psychological punishments were considered acceptable. The short, sharp shock seemed to work, and I remember no graffiti or vandalism or any trace of litter on either side of the gates. Whether or not there's a lesson to be learned there, I leave to you to decide.

~

In spite of an energetic life in and out of school, I was still piling on the weight. My family nickname was 'Podge', but nobody referred to my weight at school, or at least not to my face.

In those times fat children were very much in the minority. I can't remember anyone else at Cottage Grove being more than a little overweight, and some were painfully thin. In comparison, I was a real porker. Thanks to a combination of my mother's indulgence and my greed, I was by far the heaviest boy in my year and perhaps the whole school. This was an advantage if sticking up for myself and my mates when older bullies were about, and in playground games I was always in demand for British Bulldog or Belly Squash. But speed and agility were not my forte.

Because I was big as well as fat, the other kids didn't mock me to my face, but there was an incident which remains painfully clear and made me realise how different I was from my classmates.

It was a PE lesson, and time for a popular team game. Some benches had been turned upside down and laid out in two parallel rows. Designed for small children, the tops of the benches were no more than a foot from the floor. The idea was that competing members of each team would wiggle through the gaps and make for the far wall. Touching the wall would set the next player off.

The gap was a tight fit for a normal-sized child, and so a total no-go for me. While my skinny opponent wriggled easily through and raced to the wall, I got stuck. I couldn't get through or retreat, and was left floundering like a small beached whale.

As it was the Fifties, non-judgemental sensitivity hadn't been invented and the competitors and spectators erupted into a riot of mirth at my predicament. Being children, they made the most of it, with some kids falling to the floor in an apparent fit. The gym echoed with shrieks and yells of malicious glee as I kicked and squirmed. Worse, I could see and hear the teachers joining in the mockery.

The torment lasted until the last member of the other team reached the wall and I was freed by the PE master. In a silence broken by the occasional snigger, I put my shirt and shoes on and walked home.

Ignoring the plate of egg, chips and corned beef on the table, I pushed past my mother and made for the backyard. She found me standing in the outside toilet, the cover of the light switch in one hand and the fingers of the other pressed against the wiring. When she took me in my arms, I sobbed out my story and she realised I had been trying to kill myself rather than return to school.

I stopped her as she put on her coat to go and have words with the PE master, and persuaded her that any complaint would just make things worse. She saw that I was right, kept me home for the afternoon and comforted me with tender caresses, and, ironically, lots of food.

~

It is tempting to follow modern sensibilities and blame the bench incident for my tendency towards claustrophobia and long-term over-reaction to mockery. I don't think that's so, but it is true that in my teens I (never one to do things by halves) developed both anorexia nervosa and bulimia nervosa. This was decades before the cycles of secret starving and then binge eating and vomiting were recognised as an illness, especially not one which could affect males. I got through those pernicious and very real diseases, but still have a problem with gluttony. As with my other vices or weaknesses, I suppose I could put it down to an ancient Irish famine gene or post-war food shortages and rationing. In truth I think I have a Falstaffian attitude to life, love and food. Or, as those who know me might say, perhaps I am just a greedy bastard.

Fun and Games

In the days after the War the streets were an extension of the school playground. Games were strictly along gender divisional lines, and while girls would be on the pavement with their skirts tucked into their knickers for leapfrogging, skipping or hop-scotching, boys would command the street. It's almost unimaginable nowadays, but long games of cricket and soccer could be played with little fear of interruption by traffic.

In the school playground there would always be a game to join in. Some were single combat, others were tribal-style team games, invariably involving violence and, quite often, the spilling of blood:

Marbles is an ancient game with a variety of rules, depending on who was making them up. Hardened clay marbles have been found in Pharaoh's tombs and Aztec ruins. Even Native American Indians were hooked on them. In my day, marbles were made of glass woven through with interesting colours and patterns. The big ones were called 'alleys' apparently because they were originally made from alabaster. Like cigarette cards, conkers and religious tracts, marbles were a common medium of exchange. Games could be played on any suitable surface, though gutters were a favourite venue. I once lost an alley down a drain, and picked up the nasty skin disease of impetigo trying to fish it out.

Conkers is said to have been invented on the nearby Isle of Wight in 1848. The equipment and rules have always been pretty basic. First you made a hole through a suitably large horse chestnut with a metal skewer and threaded it on to a piece of string. Then you took it in turns to try and hit your opponent's conker. Tactics included hitting his knuckles by mistake or distracting his attention as he was about to swing. A virgin conker was known as a 'none-sy', and you gained the accumulated total of an opponent's conker when you broke it. Some champions claimed to own conkers which had accumulated hundreds of scalps, but vastly inflated claims were the norm. Sub-rules included gaining an extra go if you were the first to shout 'stringsies' when there was an entanglement. If your opponent dropped his conker, you could also claim 'stampsies' and be allowed to jump on it before the game continued. Methods of toughening up your collection included storing them for a year, baking in the oven and pickling in vinegar. In those days of at least a nod to fair play, these artificial aids to nature were frowned on, if frequently employed.

Five-stones and Jacks. Rules varied from street to street, and five stones involved scooping up dice-sized chalky cubes. Jacks was played with a ball and star-shaped metal 'stones'. The original game is said to date back to ancient Greece, when the 'ball' was a piece of rock and the stones were small sheep bones.

Cavaliers and Roundheads was, like Cops and Robbers and Cowboys and Indians no more than an excuse for a 'bundle' as we then called a brawl. Two teams were formed with players mostly choosing their preference (I was always a Cavalier, Cop or Indian). When sides had been taken, we would chase each other about on imaginary horses and lash out with imaginary swords or real fists.

Tag: There were many variations on the basic predator-prey game. In Freeze Tag, any player 'tagged' (caught) by the catcher would have to stand stock still until released by a touch from a player still at large. Another variation on a theme was Tunnel Tag. In this version, the person tagged had to stand with legs open and could only be freed by a team-mate crawling through the tunnel. This was the only form of the game I enjoyed playing with girls on our side.

Icky-Dicky was a muscular version of tag, usually reserved for boys. The essential difference was that anyone with their feet off the ground was immune from capture. This gave those pursued the excuse to climb and hang on to trees and drainpipes and railings. I remember one daredevil climbing aboard Mr Burns's bicycle to evade tagging, but retribution was swift and painful.

British Bulldog was, like Rugby Union and League, a classic male rite-of-passage game, encouraging exercise, cunning, stoicism and naked aggression. By another name the game is said to date back to Sparta when serious injuries and even death were common. In our slightly more restrained version, a single bulldog was elected at the start. For some reason it was often me, or perhaps I subconsciously put myself forward. The bulldog would stand in the middle of the field of combat and try to catch one of the mob of up to twenty players, who would rush past, through or over him, to the other end of the pitch. The first person brought down and detained would join forces with the bulldog, and this went on until the catchers had run out of catchees.

Belly Squash generated more brutality, foul play and consequent hilarity than any other male playground activity, which is probably why it was so popular. It also allowed the players to impress the female onlookers with their daring, fortitude and strength. It began with one of the two teams backing up to a strong wall. I was often chosen for this role. I liked to think it was because of my stoic resistance to pain, but more likely it was because I had the biggest and softest belly. A fellow team member would then bend over and place the top of his head against the upright boy's midriff. The remaining team members would lock on like the back halves of pantomime cows and brace themselves. The rival team members would then take turns to run up and launch themselves on to the human bench, trying to make it collapse. If it did, the vaulting team won. If the opposing team remained in place, until their attackers ran out of steam, they won.

Castle Road posse: Me with the Fitzgerald brothers and Cyril Scott. Below: With Cyril at the sixpenny swimming pool. Note the girls changing room in the background

For us kids, that distant summer of 1954 was ablaze with endless sunny days.

Or so it seemed to us, with outdoor adventures from early morning to well after dark. For most grown-ups, the season or weather didn't make a deal of difference to their daily lives.

Dads got up each weekday morning and cycled off to work at the Dockyard or local factory or building site. If there was overtime on offer, they would work the weekends too. Mums were on duty from dawn to dusk every day, and the only relief from these Groundhog Day routines would be the works outing or a week away in a boarding house at a resort just like the one they lived in.

For us kids, living in a city which was not only the nation's premier naval port but also a popular seaside resort meant we could never be bored. If we couldn't afford to spend money at the fun fair, pier or other seaside attractions, we could at least watch others enjoying themselves. Sometimes we could persuade visitors to help us join in the fun.

~

Where now stands the Sea Life centre was a popular 'children's corner', part of which was a very small boating pond. In it were half a dozen wooden motor boats of pre-war vintage. They would jostle for room and the space limitations meant you could only poodle around, but it was fun pretending to be the Commander of a motor torpedo boat or to play water-borne Dodgems till the owner ordered you out.

Near to the pond was a kiosk selling sweets, pop and

ice creams and lollies, and running alongside the prom was the miniature railway. Not only was the train in miniature, so was the length of the track, which travelled no more than couple of hundred yards alongside the seaside wall and back to the ticket office. It was a popular attraction for visitors, but our gang thought it childish and uncool.

For us and many local children, the main attraction at Children's Corner was the Sixpenny Swimming Pool. Not a lot of swimming went on as it would have been difficult to have made more than a couple of strokes on a busy day. In the summer holidays, that was nearly every day. In anything short of a thunderstorm, we would start early and get our money's worth by arriving before the gates were opened.

Mr Heywood the owner was tall and athletically-built, with thick wavy hair and white teeth emphasised by his oak-like tan. He wore little more than a pair of shorts and sandals all summer, and I remember him as a good and kindly man. He was stern when he needed to keep order, but otherwise affable and even generous. I remember one time when I lost my entry money on the way to the pool. He let me in free and even bought me an ice cream later in the day.

Our gang had its own pitch at the far end of the raised concrete seating which ran alongside the pool to the changing rooms. These were no more than open-topped wooden-walled enclosures, and we had no need of them as we would arrive in our woolly bathers with a towel round our necks and clasping a bottle of home-made ginger beer and a sandwich. But we would pretend to use the Boys enclosure so we could sneak round the back of the Girls changing room. There, we would snigger and whisper and take it in turns to put our eyes to the holes made by Big Boys and pretend we knew what we were hoping to see.

~

If we couldn't afford the swimming pool or fancied a change, Melvin, Cyril, Tinker, Tim and I might spend a long day on the beach. Equipped with a bottle of sherbet lemonade and perhaps a couple of sugar sandwiches, we would walk across the common and find a space on the stretch of shingle alongside Clarence Pier. This was a time when seaside holidays were at the height of their popularity, and a fine day would mean the beach would be packed with visitors as well as local people. The sun, beach and sea were, after all, free.

Nowadays, beach-goers arrive with enough gear to re-create their home and garden on the pebbles; in those days, they came with little and left nothing behind.

Young women would go stocking-less and wear lightweight, floral patterned dresses with a wide belt pulled tight to show off their trim figures. To watch them changing into their swimsuits under a towel was a major attraction amongst nearby males. Married and older women would be less keen on revealing what lay beneath their outer garments, and usually stuck to a paddle in the shallows with the skirt lifted to no more than knee-height. The bikini was unveiled in 1946 in, where else, Paris, but I certainly don't remember seeing one on Southsea beach in the mid-Fifties. The less inhibited young women (that is the ones with the best figures) might wear a two-piece outfit with a halter top and shorts, but a modest one-piece was the norm.

Young males would strut around in blue knitted bathers, stomachs sucked in and trying to look like Charles Atlas (ask your grandfather). When coming out of the water after a dip they would seem to be moving in slow motion. This wasn't so much for dramatic effect, but because of the weight of their sodden bathing trunks.

The only concession to the heat and location most older men would make would be to discard their coat, unhook their braces and roll up their trouser legs to mid-calf. For the older women, false teeth would be taken out and corsets loosened. I don't remember seeing a man with a knotted handkerchief on his head, but they would often sunbathe with one over the face. Where older couples gathered it could be quite like a Donald McGill postcard without the saucy bits.

Our day would be spent going in for a dip, sometimes with an old, much-patched car tyre. It was fun showing off by running into the shallows and diving through it, though the metal valve could leave a nasty scraze. As long as it stayed fairly full of air we could get a long way out to sea. If it deflated we would pretend to be drowning, though nobody ever seemed to take much notice.

On the beach we would play throwing games aimed at knocking tin cans or bottles off breakwater posts, or go treasure-hunting for any lost coins. Sometimes we would find a shilling, florin or even half-a-crown, when we would celebrate by buying ice creams from the nearest Verrecchia van.

Another popular activity was burying one of our gang in stones and sand, then pretend to have forgotten where we buried him. Building sand castles was for kids, but we would compete to flip flat stones and scallop shells through the shallows. If they hit a bather on the way, that was part of the fun.

If bored with games, we would go in search of a courting couple to embarrass or annoy. We got away with most of our pranks and it was a great time to be a boy. It was as if we were expected to misbehave. As the saying had it, boys would be boys, while little girls had to be seen to be virtuous.

Other mischievous activities would involve splashing sunbathers accidentally-on-purpose when coming out of the water, or treading on a packet of sandwiches in passing. But for all our misdeeds, we would not have been classed as bad boys. These were those who would float bottles in the shallows and throw stones to break them and leave a nasty surprise for unwary bathers. The same boys would wrap pieces of bread around stones and chuck them in the air to tempt gulls to snap them up. They would also enjoy pulling the legs off crabs or smashing their shells with a heavy stone. Sometimes the worst of them would lure a small child away from its family, then pretend to help the frantic parents in the search. They would then find the 'lost' child and hesitatingly accept a reward. Acts of casual cruelty were common then, and I suspect that is something that has not changed greatly across the years.

Our Jack Tinker was crafty rather than bad, and his favourite money-raiser on the beach was to find a likely victim and sit nearby, crying piteously until asked what was wrong. In between sobs he would say he had lost his bus fare back to Cosham and didn't know how to get home. If it worked, we would spend the proceeds on ice cream or lollies or sweets. If the grown-up offered to take him to the bus stop and pay the fare to the conductor, Jack would make an excuse and disappear to search for a more rewarding victim.

~

Although we would think of it as an uncommercial age, such concentrated gatherings of people with cash in their pockets meant there would always be something happening to part them from their money. Given how hard times were, the approaches could be less than subtle.

Overhead would often be heard the drone of a pre-war aeroplane, limping along while towing a banner advertising a brand of cigarettes or beer. Cars would cruise along the seaside road with loudspeakers advertising the circus on the common or a concert on one of the piers. On the beach, red-faced, sweaty men tramped their way across sand and shingle, encased in sandwich boards advertising local shows, cafes or bands performing at the Savoy ballroom. Floating not far off the shore would be the Daily Mirror raft, while those strolling on the promenade would run the gauntlet of any number of vendors. There would be ice cream and rock and candy-floss salesmen toting their wares in trays suspended from their shoulders. Old ladies dressed as gypsies would accost passers-by, and then there was always the Man with the Monkey. He was a cameraman who would appear to take a photograph as you approached. The theory was that you would then feel committed to pose with the monkey for a paid-for-photo. He would then take your money and address and promise to send the photo on. I often wondered how many customers got their souvenir shot of them on Southsea seafront with Mickey the Monkey.

Another regular was a man on a tricycle, carrying a board with a slogan inviting people to STOP ME & FLY ONE. If you took up the challenge, a car would run you to the airfield for a flight in a plane even older than the one towing the banner.

Charabancs would line the seafront road, promising customers run-outs to the Hampshire countryside and a historic market town like Petersfield, or even a mystery tour. It was said locally that the destination of these tours was often a mystery to the driver.

A mysterious figure trying to give rather than take money from holidaymakers was Lobby Ludd. The original character had been created by a newspaper in the 1920s and was later revived by the *Daily Mail*. The resorts he would be visiting were announced, and the only clue was that he would be carrying a rolled-up copy of the newspaper. If you thought you had spotted him, you had to approach while waving your copy of the *Mail* and say: 'You are Lobby Ludd and I claim my five pounds'. Being too young we didn't qualify, but would amuse ourselves by approaching the most unlikely people, accusing him or her (and once, I remember, a Carmelite nun) of being Lobby Ludd and demanding a fiver. It never worked but, as Tinker Jackson said, it was worth trying as one day some loony might actually give us the money.

Another seafront attraction was the skating rink. It was circular and with the silver-painted central dome and sloping roof it looked rather as if a flying saucer had landed on Southsea Common.

The rink was a popular attraction for local children, visitors and especially sailors having a boozy runashore. Like the beach, it was always crowded, and I think whoever invented the dangerous sport of Rollerball may well have got the idea from a visit to our skating rink in the 1950s.

Apart from the number of people going in various directions with different levels of ability, sobriety and sense of balance, a constant danger was the irregularity of the skating surface. It was made of sheets of asbestos-like material, and the joints had moved over the years. On a busy day the clicking of hundreds of wheels as they passed over the raised joints sounded like an invasion by a host of giant crickets.

The cracks and protruding edges were a particular hazard to beginners - and especially those who'd hired a pair of roller skates with a sticky wheel. This was a common fault, and a sudden seizing-up could throw the wearer off balance and cause a major pile-up.

Another hazard was the snack bar, which was a railed-off section with a narrow exit and entrance. Getting to it was as tricky and potentially dangerous as trying to leave a busy motorway when in the outside lane.

If you made it safety, you could have a cup of Oxo or a snack and watch the carnage while betting on who would go over next and how badly they would be hurt. Yet another potential pile-up hazard arose when skaters stopped off, then took a hot drink, steak pie or ice cream with them as they re-joined the melee. It was perhaps the original form of eating on the go and could have serious consequences.

Like any ballroom, the rink attracted the serious practitioners and show-offs as well as we hopeless amateurs. They were marked out by having their own expensive skating boots and a very superior manner.

On certain days the central section would be roped off and the proper skatists would perform for our benefit. It was a very early version of *Strictly Come Dancing*, and the participants were just as over-the-top. The women and even the children would wear pancake makeup that stood out from their faces like the lumpy bits on a Van Gogh painting. They would sport helmet-like beehive hairstyles and tight costumes with multi-layered, frilly ballet-dancer-style skirts.

The males would sport heavily Brylcreemed quiffs and be squeezed into tight trousers and shirts with voluminous sleeves. Together or solo, the experts would take dramatically to the floor and glide around to the tinny strains of Swan Lake or an unsuitable pop song.

I was a regular spectator at these demonstrations, but not to admire the skills and grace of the performers. I was there to sit in open-mouthed worship of Susan Peacock.

She was a petite, pretty dark-haired girl of about my age, with snub nose and flashing (it seemed to me) dark eyes. Her looks, outfit and graceful performance made me her slave. I don't think we ever spoke, but she was the love of my life for all that long, hot summer.

~

Across the road at the Rock Gardens, we might stop to take in the travelling Guinness Show. There would be giant posters, one featuring a cheery man carrying a huge steel girder on one shoulder to demonstrate just how good the stout was for you. Others would show the famous toucan balancing a glass of Guinness on his beak, and a bemused zoo keeper looking at an ostrich with a glass stuck half-way down its neck. Southsea was also one of the few resorts to be visited by the Guinness Clock. Created to mark the Festival of Britain in 1951, it was a Heath-Robinson type contraption more than twenty feet high, with music and moving parts and towers and doors opening to reveal the Guinness animals and children's books characters like the Mad Hatter. It might not sound much to modern ears, but it was a thing of wonder to a whole generation.

~

Next stop on our long day's journey along the prom would be South Parade Pier.

At low tide it was a challenge to climb up the seaweed and barnacle-covered ancient iron legs, climb over the railings and walk casually past the attendants back to the prom. At high tide it was good sport for the most daring to swim out and tug the lines of anglers so they would think they had caught a fish. It was a dangerous game as the prankster risked becoming the catch. Tinker Jackson claimed to have once put a piece of ready-battered and fried cod on a hook but nobody believed he would waste such a luxury just to give a fisherman a shock.

Over the road from the pier was the Canoe Lake, which was kept topped up by a pipe running under the prom and into the sea. There were no canoes but there was a collection of old rowing boats. They were hired out and the man with the concession really did call out 'Come in number Seven, your time is up!'

A popular activity for small children was crabbing. All you needed was a jam jar suspended from a length of string and a crust of bread for bait. The small green crabs we caught were inedible, so mostly went free.

Another diversion was watching the model boats. There would sometimes be a Jetex or petrol-powered little speedboat, but mostly it was the grace and silent beauty of sail as old men played at being captain of a giant four-rigger.

~

The end of a long day.

Dusk would be falling and we would hang on to see the illuminations come on. These were mainly strings of painted lightbulbs which had survived the attention of stone-throwing, catapult and peashooter-shooting boys. But on the lampposts were set out a number of state-of-the-art animated figures. Movement was suggested by the lights going on and off in sequence, and favourites were a cowboy with a lasso and a dog with a wagging tail and a smoking cigarette in its mouth.

Tired but content, we would set off home across the Common. In those different days it was generally safe for children to be abroad, and I don't remember feeling fearful on the darkest night. Sailors and Teddy Boys might fight each other or themselves, but children went unmolested by strangers.

Busy beach. A typical scene on a sunny summers day

Credit Pete Brown, Do you Remember in Portsmouth

Charge of the Bike Brigade

Credit Memories of Bygone Portsmouth

Navy Days

At last count there were forty-seven commissioned ships in a Navy which once ruled the waves around the world. One of the most evocative reminders of those days of Empire is HMS Victory, Nelson's flagship at the Battle of Trafalgar, she now lies in honourable retirement in Portsmouth's Naval Base. It is said that not a scrap of the original woodwork remains, but at least the old ship occupies the same space it has filled for more than two centuries.

At the 1953 Coronation Fleet Review, more than one hundred and ninety Royal Naval warships paraded off Spithead. In those days we still liked to think of ourselves as the most powerful navy in the world, and the Pompey dockyard as the best in Britain, and with some reason.

Around 20,000 men (and a number of women) were employed in the 'Yard and if - as they said - you kept your nose clean it could be a job for life. An apprentice shipwright would start on £1. 16s. 3d a week and was granted a full week's holiday a year. Many of the jobs were semi-skilled or unskilled and it was said that some Dockyard Mateys did no more than turn up for work and look busy. In later life I spent an afternoon wandering around the Dockyard to win a bet. On advice from a seasoned matey I wore a dirty pair of overalls and carried a length of rope, a piece of metal pipe and a spanner. If anyone looked at me I'd just need to step out lively and look as if I knew where I was going. But not too quickly, he cautioned, as it would look suspicious to see anyone hurrying anywhere in the Yard. It worked, and the only time I was in danger came when The Charge of the Bike Brigade began.

~

At knocking-off time, a surging tide of humanity would spew out from the massive Unicorn gate, with the majority of the tens of thousands of Dockyard workers mounted on bicycles. Anxious to get home to tea, the horde would literally stop the traffic, and paid no heed to the rules of the road. Through the streets they would rampage, peeling off to their homes with a cheery wave to workmates and a two-fingered salute for any drivers or pedestrians who believed they had the right of way.

The spectacle was so impressive it was said that locals and visitors would gather just to see the vast host emerge. The event even inspired a common popular saying when someone walked out of a public toilet without buttoning his fly. 'Watch it mate,' a helpful male passer-by would warn, 'Your dockyard gates are open. They might let something dangerous out...'

~

The area around the Dockyard main gates became even busier when a big ship docked. If it were a Royal Navy vessel back after a long spell at sea, publicans within a mile of the Dockyard would double their beer orders. If it were a giant American aircraft carrier with thousands of mostly young, relatively well-heeled and randy males on board, it could be hard to move for young and not-so-young ladies in fake leopard-skin coats, high heels and overdone make-up.

When the local working girls had more than enough on their hands, their numbers would be supplemented by colleagues from further afield. If a number of foreign and

British ships were in port, it was said that extra trains from London would be laid on.

For us, the arrival of a foreign ship was almost as much of an attraction as it would be to the local working girls. It wasn't uncommon to see small boys and painted ladies jostling for attention as the visiting crews came out of the gates for their runashore. They would be there to make a living; we would be there to cadge a cigarette, cap badge or tally (hat band).

'Got any gum chum?' was the call if it was an American ship, and it was surprisingly often rewarded with a stick or even a whole packet. When it was a Russian ship, the most prized scrounge was a small gold and red metal badge with hammer-and-sickle on it. I still have one, swapped for a stick of Yankee gum and a single Turf cigarette with a young, fresh-faced Russian sailor. I think I got the better of the bargain, and when I look at it on my desk I wonder how his life turned out. The little stars were given added value as Russian sailors were not often seen on the street without an escort. It was even said that they would be taken on official sightseeing tours organised by the on-board representative of the CCCP. The hired coaches would drive around the city with blinds down when going through affluent areas like Southsea, and lifted to show the poorer and bomb-damaged parts of Portsmouth.

~

Long before the Gunwharf Quays arrived, a more modest centre of entertainment in this part of Old Portsmouth was the bridge leading from the Hard to the Gosport Ferry. At low tide, crowds would gather to watch the mudlarks at work. The rules were simple. Spectators would throw coins from the bridge, and barefoot and ragged urchins from the Portsea slums would scrabble to find them. It was anything but good clean fun, and sometimes blood would mingle with the mud when a drunken sailor would throw a high value coin over the railings. I remember it as an almost Dickensian scene, but it was how things were then. Nowadays it would be seen as a degrading spectacle, but back then a few pennies won for scrabbling and fighting in the mud was seen as a good reward.

After watching and even feeling a little envious of the mudlarks, we'd usually leave the Hard and wander through the narrow streets of tall, imposing houses built for wealthy families as the town prospered. Ironically, some of those now stupendously priced homes clustered around the Cathedral were near-slum dwellings for the Portsea poor in the middle of the 20th century. Much later, the tenants were shuttled off to Portsea, while their former homes were transformed and given pretentious names like Trade Winds or Nelson House. Nowadays there's a chasm between Portsea and Old Portsmouth, but back then it was not so.

This part of the city was definitely not our territory, but we would generally be given safe passage as Pompey locals. If not, we would take to our heels. The Portsea Boys were known to be an especially tough bunch.

Beyond the Cathedral we'd pause to look up at the bust of Charles the First in its niche in the Square Tower and consider Tinker Jackson's claim that it was in fact the king's real head, dipped in cement after his execution for betraying his country and helping the Germans in the First World War.

After a visit to the Hot Walls and an argument as to how it got its name, we'd walk along the prom, past the Moat and our secret gang HQ. It was about here that we'd pause like Bisto Kids (ask your grandmother) to scent the air and inhale the bouquet of freshly cooked doughnuts, fried onions, candy floss, stale beer, cigarette smoke and body odour.

Southsea fun fair is perhaps not that exciting for children used to Disneyland and Thorpe Park, but in 1954 it was almost a place of wonder. Here we would find dramatic colours, lights and sounds, shot through with screams which were sometimes of genuine terror. During the day the fun fair was a noisy and exciting place. After dark it became almost Dante-esque.

The fright factor was how many of the customers rated the rides. In spite of the unearthly moans, rattling chains, plastic skeletons and the fairground worker in a sheet who leaped out on you in the Ghost Train tunnel was pretty tame and, we thought, more suitable for girls. It would probably have scored no more than a two out of ten on our ranking. Other rides were far more nerve-jangling, sometimes unintentionally so.

A long-established attraction, the Big Wheel looked like a sedate ride, but often swayed and wobbled worryingly as if working its way loose from the giant rusty retaining nuts and bolts. The wobble and occasional groan of tortured metal was generally seen as part of the fun and an excuse for taking a tighter hold on your girlfriend. The wheel also got stuck regularly, marooning passengers for up to an hour. This was another bonus for courting couples, but not so much fun for older people in a strong wind with the gondola creaking and swaying. Drunken sailors would see a hold-up as an opportunity for showing off by climbing hand-over-hand down the framework to the ground, or even by dropping from one gondola to those below.

The Dodgem rink was a contest to hit rather than miss other cars, and nowadays would have been bankrupted by claims for whiplash or mental trauma suffered by the customers. Nearby on the Lightning Swirl, passengers were mostly kept from following the natural laws of gravity and inertia by the wobbly safety bar across the open pods. Skilful use of the pedal brake could make them pause and then go into a sudden rotation which would have sickened an experienced astronaut.

Then there was the Chair-O-Plane, a sort of elevated roundabout with bench seats on creaking cables flying out almost horizontally at top speed.

Worth at least a seven on the scare scale were the two gaudily-painted, rivet-studded metal carriages which swung on arms up to the top of their loop before whizzing down like some monstrous and infernal Victorian steam engine.

Nowadays, passengers' mobile phones would plummet to the ground at the top of the swing. In those days they often lost the contents of their stomachs. That's why there was always a clear space around the perimeter.

When in town, one of the most impressive sideshows was the Wall of Death. This was a huge upright wooden cylinder in which motor-cyclists would whiz around, held on by centrifugal force. Then there was the Sticky Wall, which would probably score a nine on the scare scale for most people. It too was a giant cylinder, with a set of steps for passengers to climb to the top. Once inside, they stood with backs to the wall as the cylinder began to slowly rotate. When it was well under way, the floor would simply drop away, leaving the passengers hopefully stuck to the wall. I never saw anyone actually plummet to the bottom, but lots of spectators would ring the top in hopeful expectation of seeing an accident of one sort or another.

Because of the cost, the rides were mostly spectator sports for us, but there were the machines if you had a penny to spare. If you had the funds, there were the stalls. To win at Hoopla, you had only to toss a wooden hoop over the stand on which the prize stood. The stallholder would regularly demonstrate how easily the hoops would fit over the stands, but I suspect he used one which was bigger than the standard issue.

Then there was the archery stall and rifle range for young bucks to impress their girlfriends, and for younger customers the Lucky Duck where you used a small rod and line to try to hook a plastic duck. If you were successful and found it had a number stuck to the bottom you won a prize, which was often a goldfish in leaky plastic bag. As with the Hoopla game, the stallholder would regularly show how easy it would be to win by holding up a handful of lucky bottoms before putting the ducks back into the water, but I reckon he was practiced at sleight of hand.

One of the most popular stalls was run by a regular guest at our lodging house. A cheerful man with a lot of gold teeth, I never saw Mr Brown without his cheese cutter-style cap even when emerging from our posh new bathroom wearing nothing else but a towel round his waist. He was a travelling showman of the old school, and he and his wife arrived to set up and run the Penny Roll every summer. Quite simply, the challenge was to roll a penny down a slot onto the board, which was divided into squares marked with various amounts from tuppence to a mighty half-crown. If your coin landed within a winning square without touching the lines around it, you got your money back plus the prize amount. Like modern-day fairground games of similar type, the positioning and amount of prize squares must have been carefully worked out to make the odds in favour of the operator.

I was a regular visitor to the Penny Roll; not so much because I thought I'd win a prize, but because I might see the Browns' daughter.

I still didn't know exactly why, but, like Susan Peacock at the Skating Rink, I found Mandy Brown disturbingly appealing. Like Susan, she was petite and around my age, but fair-haired and pretty in a big-eyed elfin-like way. When she was behind the counter with her parents I would spend hours hanging around, trying to impress her by wasting all my spare pennies just to win a smile.

Popular machine games invited you to drop a coin in at the top and manipulate its progress down to a winning slot. Then there was a horse-racing game where you frantically turned a handle to try and be the first to cross the winning line. But most memorable to me of all the entertainments was the laughing sailor. He was an animated dummy with a maniacal smile and the most chilling and unfunny laugh you could imagine. When you put your penny in, the figure would flail its arms and give out a high-pitched cackle. Tinker Jackson said the laugh was a recording of a particularly loony patient at St James Asylum in Milton, and it wasn't hard to believe him.

~

Southsea fun fair was owned by the sort of uneducated but shrewd and determined character who seemed to prosper in the post-war days. It may have been no more than coincidence, but many of those clever, hard-bitten entrepreneurs in the world of mass entertainment seemed to come short and stout and rough of hand and manner. A further coincidence was that three of them also shared the same name. There was Billy Butlin and his holiday camps, Billy Smart and his circus, and, in our part of the country, Billy Manning and his fun fair.

I only ever saw the great man at a distance, sitting in an old armchair outside the massive trailer home parked behind the fair. It was said he lived in the trailer because he liked to hear the yells and screams and whoops of people enjoying themselves and, most importantly, spending their money. In his later years he shocked the Southsea Establishment by buying what had once been the poshest hotel in Southsea. According to the blurb on the current owners' website, Billy was refused entrance to the Queens Hotel in the late 1960s so bought the place, sacked the staff and moved in. I prefer the story that he bought the Queens mainly to put two fingers up to Portsmouth's *beau monde*. I don't know which version was true, but I like to think of him sitting at a window on the third floor, looking across the common at his fun fair while smiling at what the punters downstairs would pay for an exotic cocktail in the Brandy Bubble bar.

The Round Tower, 'Hot Walls' and Sallyport

Credit Patrick Boyle, Memories of Bygone Portsmouth

There was a brief distraction from my most golden of summers when I had my tonsils removed.

It was believed that taking them out would avoid sore throats and related complications in later years. This was proved to be decidedly not so, but in the 1950s it was almost a rite of passage. I left mine at Southsea's specialist Eye and Ear hospital, which was perhaps why they made a bit of a mess of taking my tonsils out.

If you want to get an idea of what the NHS was like in those early days, you have to remember the country's recent history and zietgeist or mood and general attitudes. Matrons really were like Hatti Jacques in the *Carry On* films and patients were supposed to lie still, do what they were told and clear off as soon as they could walk. Anything less than a lost limb and you were likely to be told to pull yourself together and think of people who were really ill and had something to complain about. That's not to say the nurses and doctors didn't care or were particularly insensitive; they had just learned in recent years that a stiff upper lip and a brusque manner was sometimes the best way to deal with the times and casualties.

I don't remember anything before the operation, but have a vivid memory of coming to on a mattress seemingly filled with bombsite rubble. On the locker beside the bed was an enamelled bowl, filled to the brim with blood.

I remember my throat being sore for a while, and recently saw a report saying the fashion for tonsillectomies had been a waste of time. In fact, rather than preventing future ailments it could cause them. People who have had their tonsils out are three times more likely to suffer from infectious or upper respiratory tract diseases which include asthma, influenza, chronic obstructive disease and pneumonia.

Over the years I've managed to collect most of those, but I guess it's a bit late to sue for medical negligence. Anyway, at the time I thought the experience worth it to be able to regale my gang with stories about basins of blood and seeing patients with no arms or legs or even heads. There was also the exquisite delight of being spoiled rotten by all the nurses and living on a diet of ice cream for a fortnight. I also remember my dad giving me a cuddle in the family bed, which was the last time I recall us making such close physical contact.

The sunny summer ran lazily on, and business was booming at Castle Road.

With a full house, John and I were relegated to sleeping on put-you-up beds in the shed with the dog and cat. For me it was an adventure and I'd wear my Davey Crocket outfit to bed and pretend we were in a log cabin. John wasn't so pleased as the lack of mirrors hindered his practice at creating the perfect Duck's Arse.

We were not the only family members to be inconvenienced by the need to make money while the sun shone. It was not uncommon for our parents to doss down in the kitchen, while if Uncle Bill was ashore he would sleep in the dining room.

Our regulars were always sure of accommodation, but Mother certainly thought less of the B&B customers. I think this was because they understandably wanted to get maximum value for their money. Sometimes this meant sneaking off with a towel or tea spoon or the remains of a bar of soap. I remember my mother storming into the kitchen almost incandescent with rage when a family from Birmingham were having breakfast. He and his wife were images from a McGill picture-postcard; he was a jolly, round man and she was even rounder. The children were obviously doing their best to follow in their parent's footsteps and lose sight of their feet before long.

'What's the matter, beloved?' queried my dad as Mother crashed the frying pan on the stove.

'I asked them if they'd like some more breakfast...' snorted Mother, 'and they said yes!'

'So why did you ask them?' I asked, genuinely puzzled.

'I was just being polite,' she said in icy tones. 'People are supposed to say "no thank you", not "yes, please"'.

I didn't get her point, but agreed with her that our regular guests were much more interesting than the B &B customers. How and where else would you get to meet a travelling escapologist who regularly locked himself in the bathroom, or a circus lion tamer who was afraid of our cat?

~

As a perfect summer drew to a close, I'd sit contentedly on the prom with my gang, looking out to sea thinking and talking about how lucky we were. Our parents had come through the War and, though our city had been knocked about a bit, things were relatively good. We knew how horrific it had been for so many people, and how so many of Portsmouth's sons did not come home from sea and land. We lived in a time of what we saw as plenty, within a close community and in tight families. We didn't know much about the rest of the world except that people were starving in India so we should think ourselves lucky and clear our plates.

Life was so much simpler then, and, I believe, better for it in many ways. Given the choice of living then and now, I think I would happily forego the wonders and attractions of fitted bathrooms and carpets, central heating and - especially - social media celebs and oven chips.

It might just be inevitable nostalgia for times long gone, but with life so bounteous now compared to our day, I just wonder why there are so many mental health and emotional 'issues'. Most of all, I wonder why so many people in this time and place of milk and honey look so bloody miserable.

I knew something was up when Mother took my hand and led me into the front room. It was worrying as the only time this happened was when I was in trouble or there was bad news.

Every now and then a local shopkeeper or parent would allege I had damaged their property or son, and I would be summoned to a show trial in front of the complainant. Mother would give me a dressing-down and I would apologise for any distress caused and promise it would never happen again. Served with tea and sympathy and cake or a nip of Uncle Bill's pussers' rum and mollified by Mother's performance, the complainant would usually be content. Sometimes they would even ask my mother not to be too hard on me, as keeping me indoors for a week or stopping my pocket money for a month seemed excessive. Once, the manager of a shop in Elm Grove even slipped me a tanner as he left to make up for the severity of my alleged punishment. David Greig was a posh grocery store, and the small, timid manager a natural target for our gang. We would never have thought of stealing anything, but would make faces through the window or bow in mock-reverence to rich ladies seated in the cool interior while their order was being made up. Another prank was to wait till the coast was clear and sidle in and ask a new assistant if there were any broken biscuits. If the answer was yes, we would say he or she should have been more careful with them, blow a raspberry and then leg it. Hardly big-time anti-social behaviour even in those days, but enough to bring about physical retribution if we were caught. Adults were not afraid to give a child a ticking-off or even a cuff about the ears for what was filed under the general heading of 'sauce' or 'cheek'. In the rare case of a policeman arriving to tell the parents about their child's misbehaviour, neighbouring curtains would twitch in unison and the rest of the street would know the shocking details within hours. Of course we can't turn the clock back and we are where we are, but direct action in the form of verbal or physical chastisement from a teacher, bobby or even passing stranger did seem to do the trick and keep us kids in line. Children and even adults were constantly reminded of their moral and social duties and responsibilities in many ways, including gossip and comments about neighbours, and even a doorstep not being as well-honed as it should be. National Service was in part aimed to teach young adults that they were not as important as they might otherwise have thought, and that there was always a cost to kicking out against the rules.

~

The reason Mother had called me into the front room was not because of a complaint against me or my gang, or to break the news of a death or disaster. To my immature and self-centred young mind, what she had to tell me was worse than any death or disaster. We would soon, she said, be leaving Castle Road and moving to another part of the city.

I remember with real clarity how anxiously she watched and waited for my reaction. She knew how happy I was and what a big thing a small move away from friends and familiar surroundings could be for a ten-year-old child.

It took a moment for what she said to sink in, and when it did my only question was 'Why?'

As Mother knew, Castle Road was the centre of my world. My friends lived here, my school was just down the road and I was surrounded by my favourite sweet shops and bomb-dumps. The seaside with the beaches, fun fair and all the other attractions were a mile away across Southsea Common. Then there were all our interesting lodgers. Why would she or anyone want to leave such a place?

Thinking of what I'd be leaving behind filled my eyes with tears, which caused the same thing to happen to Mother. She pulled me close and said she knew I would be sad for a while, but it was time to move on...and we would not be travelling far. With the lettings and extra jobs dad and herself (I think she actually meant herself) had saved enough to buy a place that would be our own.

It was the first time I realised that we didn't own 26 Castle Road. As Mother said, it was our home but not our house. She had bought an empty shop in a part of Portsmouth called Milton. It wasn't far away and I'd be able to finish my last year at Cottage Grove and see my friends regularly. I'd make new ones in my new home, and there would be new adventures and new places to explore.

I sniffed and looked up at her concerned face and thought about what she had said, and gradually things began to look better.

They looked even better when Mother told me that the new family business would be a sweet shop.

I'm sitting on the grassy slope above the Castle Road Knights' secret HQ.

The gulls and terns have flown to wherever they spend their nights, dusk is falling and the fun fair is in full swing. Above the crashes, swooshes and rattles and shouts and screams I can hear the maniacal laughter of the mechanical drunken sailor. Perhaps he has heard the news and is mocking me because I have to leave this magic place.

I stand, try to skip a flat stone more than four dips across the turning tide, fail and start the walk home. There's a sweet sadness in my heart, but also a feeling of growing anticipation and even excitement.

I know, as Mother said, there will be new adventures to come and I will still be having them in Portsmouth. Young as I am, I know how lucky and privileged to live in my city by the sea for a heartbeat of its rich and sometimes turbulent life. I also know that wherever I go and whatever I do, I will always come home.

As we locals like to say, Portsmouth is a hard place to escape from, and in my heart I will always be a Pompey Boy.

Acknowledgements

When I started my research for this book, I planned to give credit to everyone who responded to my on-line queries and surveys about their memories of Portsmouth in the 1950s. In practice, the list tallied more than three hundred before I even got properly started. All those kind enough to respond to my surveys and volunteer priceless details will know who they are. My sincere thanks to you all. Photographs have been credited where possible.

A particularly important source was the addictive Memories of Bygone Portsmouth, created and run by the indefatigable JJ Marshallsay:

Other sources include:

Portsmouth Past and Present:
Portsmouth Past and Present

History in Portsmouth - The Cooper Allen Music Archive
historyinportsmouth.co.uk/events/cooper-allen/1949.htm

DO YOU REMEMBER IN PORTSMOUTH (FACEBOOK)

A brief History of Southsea by Tim Lambert
http://www.localhistories.org/southsea.html

The Portsmouth History Centre
/libraries/portsmouth-history-centre-and-records-office

The Popular Music Portsmouth Scene
http://michaelcooper.org.uk/C/pmsindex.htm

A Tale of One City
http://www.ataleofonecity.portsmouth.gov.uk/gallery/

According to one website, there are precisely ninety-seven novels and non-fiction works about or set in Portsmouth. Make that a round hundred, as the list does not include the first three of the Inspector Mowgley Murder Mystery series, written by no other than me.

The list can be found here:

https://www.mappit.net/bookmap/places/341/portsmouth-england-gb/

One of the books is 'Pompey', by Jonathan Meades, published by Vintage Books. It deals with the same era as this memoir, and has been acknowledged as a modern masterpiece. Potential customers should be advised it is not easy reading, and was described by critics as both brilliant and disgusting. A bit like the things people say about our city, then.

Sneak Preview

We hope you enjoyed the first volume of Just a Pompey Boy. The next tranche starts as the East family move from their quirky lodging house in Southsea to a failed corner shop in Milton. Meanwhile, George Snr becomes the proprietor of an even more failed snooker hall. Here's a sample of Volume Two of *Just a Pompey Boy*.

More information at www.george-east.net

~

The next month sped by as my parents got ready to open the doors of Kay's Stores.

Sensibly, the division of labour was that my dad was responsible for the DIY, painting and bodging and heavy lifting work, while Mother would be dealing with the business side of things.

I was serving my final term at Cottage Grove, commuting by bus and spending time after school on my beloved bombsite adventure playgrounds, a facility noticeably absent in Milton.

One evening I arrived home to find a strange man eating a tin of cat food and pretending to like it. He wasn't barking mad, but a salesman who wanted to show how wholesome his product was. I felt sorry for him when Mother let him finish the tin before saying she had already done a deal with the man from Whiskas.

Meanwhile, shelves were being put up and everything painted, including my father. He wasn't much of a hand with a saw or a brush, but as mother said, he was very cheap and easily bullied.

Outside, the newly-painted shop front was a gleaming combination of bright blue, deep green and muddy brown and a very red red. This was not a design feature aiming to attract maximum attention, but the using-up of a lot of half-empty tins from the shed at Castle Road.

Above the main window, the name of my parents' new adventure had been boldly proclaimed in the bright blue, augmented with banana yellow. Again, money had been saved by letting dad do the signage. As he had never written any signs and was no great hand at writing letters, the project was more or less doomed from the outset. As usual, dad hadn't done much pre-planning or laying-out of the lettering but got stuck straight in with a two-inch brush. This meant the letters got smaller and closer together towards the end, and the 'y' in *Kay's Stores* lost its tail. Several passers-by stopped to ask who Kav was, which my mother used as an opportunity to steer them into the shop to meet the great man. I think the creators of *Open All Hours* may have got their inspiration from my mother.

I don't know what the original plan was, but the final choice of what the shop would sell seemed based on a mixture of circumstance, availability and budget.

Fratton Park was less than a mile away and with no competition in the immediate vicinity and thousands of people passing by or near the shop on match days, what basics should be included in the offerings was, as they say nowadays, a no-brainer. There was no licence for newspapers, but Kay's was allowed to sell cigarettes. Confectionery, soft drinks and snacks were a must, and on match days Mother even laid out a window display of rosettes and badges and other Portsmouth FC favours. She knew that an army of fans would pass the window before arriving outside the ground where the favours were officially on sale. She was also canny enough to post me or dad as look-outs in case rival fans made their noisy way towards the shop. In that case, the Pompey favours would be swiftly removed from the window and ones more to the liking of the away supporters would be produced from under the counter as the fans ordered their packets of Woodbines or Weights fags and steak pies or pork and dripping rolls.

Kay's would also be selling tinned goods and groceries and anything else which could be crammed into the available space. The only comestibles not on offer were fruit and vegetables. This was ostensibly so as not to tread on the toes of the greengrocer next door, but mostly because Mother had seen how little profit there was in a pound of spuds and a rapidly wilting lettuce. Apart from Mr Weekes our bear-like but amiable neighbour, the only other shop was at the other end of Frensham Road. Barely visible through the grubby window was a half-hearted display of some tired-looking balls of wool and faded pre-war knitting patterns.

As usual, Mother had proved her ability to do her homework, see what an area was missing, and provide it.

~

After stocking the shop to the limit of her budget and filling any empty shelf space with empty sweet tins and fake packets of cigarettes, Mother was ready for the grand opening.

I remember my dad cautiously testing out the till, which was definitely of pre-war vintage, and probably pre-World War One. It looked like something you would see on the counter of a Dickensian haberdashery store, was made of wood and shaped like a miniature coffin. At one end was a brass handle to pull the drawer out and on the top was a glass panel with a slot in it, giving access to a roll of paper. The idea was to write down the amount of each transaction, then open the drawer. A little bell would ring and the paper reel would move on a fraction. It was noticeable how rarely either my mother or father actually noted down a sale or the amount taken for it. As Mother said when I asked her about it, she and dad were the only two using the till and she had a very good memory so it would be a waste of paper to note the transactions.

~

As she was the proprietor, Mother refused to wear an apron or overall, and always opened the shop looking as if she was off on a swish night out. She rightly figured it would gain respect from the female customers, and admiration from the men. Both would help up the takings, she reckoned. When on duty in the evenings, Dad would wear a white coat of the sort barbers and scientists wore, and had written the name of the shop on the top pocket in red ink. It had soaked into the material and wasn't very legible, but at least there was room to complete the loop on the 'y' in Kay's Stores.

In those days, advertising was very much a low-key affair for local businesses, and the announcement of the opening was limited to a hand-made poster in the window. My mother, being who she was, also knocked on every door in Frensham Road and beyond, introducing herself and telling the potential customers what would be on special offer for the first week of opening.

I of course didn't know how well the business was doing, but the bell on the top of the door seemed to jangle regularly and once they were in, it wasn't easy to leave without a purchase, even if they had rushed in to ask to use the phone because of an emergency at home. Like Arkwright in *Open All Hours* or Auntie Wainwright in the junk shop in *Last of the Summer Wine*, Mother was very good at not letting customers leave without taking more than they had come in for.

~

Although the shop seemed to be going well, it wasn't long before Mother suggested my dad looked for a day job. He would take over to give Mother a break throughout opening hours and proved popular with the customers. With his height, dark good looks and ready wit, I think Mother sometimes thought he was a bit too popular with the female customers of a certain age. Looking back, I suspect she was torn between the irritation of seeing dad's lady fans fawn over him, and pleasure at the value of the extra income he could coax out of an admirer.

Whatever the motivation, dad found or was found a job as a bread and cakes roundsman for a local bakery. This was another shrewd move by Mother, as Kay's Stores was a customer of Dyke's bakery, and dad delivered her order at the end of his round. I don't think Mother would have allowed actual larceny, but I know there were always lots of past-their-best fancy cakes and buns and loaves on show in the shop. They were sold at reduced prices, and I suspect the price to Mother was extremely favourable.

~

My time at Cottage Grove was coming to an end, the 11-plus Examination loomed and I would soon be making another move from familiar, comfortable surroundings. At our last meeting before the end of term, the Castle Road Knights voted unanimously that I should continue to be a full member no matter where I lived for the rest of my life. In an emotional moment we swore that nothing would break our bond, though once again we chickened out from sealing the oath with our blood.

It was a solemn moment and whatever we said or promised, I think that we all realised that leaving Cottage Grove meant we were moving towards childhood's end.

~

Life went on in those final weeks, but I was bemused how the girls in our class seemed the most upset at our imminent parting. Some of them would come to see me on the bus or bike after school, and Samantha Stott (she of the front bottom) would actually pedal the three miles several times a week to bring me a bag of sweets.

When I asked my mother why she thought that a girl would cycle all that way to give a bag of sherbet lemons to a boy who lived in a sweet shop, she smiled, then said, as I'd find out when I grew up, girls were not, in some respects, at all like boys.

Match of the Day

On alternate Saturdays you could hear the roar from Fratton Park as if it was just across the road, which in fact it was.

On match days, tens of thousands would descend on Portsmouth FC's home ground hours before kick-off. Looking back I see it as a sort of Lowry-esq painting, except that amongst the drab clothes and cloth caps would be the black hats and tally bands of sailors. As none but a handful of ratings would be natives of Portsmouth and most from north of the Watford Gap, the cheering for a goal by the away team would sometimes equal that of a Pompey strike. Strangely, the drawn-out oooohs in reaction to a near-miss from either side would be almost as loud as the cheers for a goal.

Every home match, confectionery, snack and cigarette sales would rocket. Chocolate bars, cakes and filled rolls would fly off the shelves, sometimes literally if Mother and dad were under pressure behind the counter. Cheese rolls would be on sale at Fratton Park, but the regulars knew what they would taste like. And the tea and snack bar was quite near to the truly odiferous toilet block.

On the day before the game, Mother would roast a big leg of pork and Dad would bring home an extra couple of trays of crusty bread rolls. The next morning the rolls would be buttered with the dripping and filled with a thick slice of fatty pork. Lots of pepper and salt would be added, and lucky customers might find a piece of crackling as a bonus.

Although I was never a football fan, I'd feel the air of anticipation and excitement in the streets as kick-off time approached. Soccer had arrived in the town in the mid-19th century with dockers and sailors from the North.

Portsmouth FC was founded in 1898 and had never moved from its original ground at Frogmore Road. And we were a top team.

After a mixed history of results, Pompey had won the FA cup in 1939 and the Division One title for two consecutive years from 1948-50. Now the team was riding high and enjoying what would be later known as their 'glory days'. The record attendance was a massive 51,385, and an average crowd would exceed 35,000. That meant good business for shops near the ground, which was one of the reasons dad had suggested to Mother that we should move to Frensham Road and set up shop. Dad and John were big fans and would hurry to the ground after the rush was over, and sometimes they would take me along.

For a ten-year-old hanging on to his father and brother's hands, it was an experience to be swept along in the midst of an ever-swelling crowd, the air thick with cigarette smoke, beery fumes, chants and shouts and the crackle of rattles and hoots from hooters and horns. In those pre-deodorant days, the smell of the crowd would probably have rivalled the roar, but we were all the same so few would have noticed.

Programme and rosette and souvenir sellers marked the route, each displaying their wares on a board fixed to a long pole like a Roman Legionnaire holding the Eagle proudly aloft.

There would be a police presence lining the route from Fratton Station but physical violence was rare even though the away fans were allowed to mingle with home supporters. In fact, there was usually more violence on the field than off it, especially if Jimmy Scoular was playing.

Having paid then squeezed through the turnstile, dad and John would take no notice of the stewards with their long lollipop sticks showing where there were spaces, and shove their way to their favoured station on the half-way line. As there was no seating for the rank-and-file supporters, they would lean against a metal barrier similar to an oversized bike rack. I would be shepherded with other small children down to the cinder surround. There we could sit and watch the action, play five-stones, swap cigarette cards or throw handfuls of coke at each other.

Whenever I think back to those long-gone Saturday afternoons I see the scene in black and white. Along with the sailors, civilians would be uniformly dressed in drab shades. The men would be wearing grey gaberdine mackintoshes, woollen overcoats or donkey jackets over grey flannels and black shoes. These with heads covered would be wearing rumpled cloth caps or, occasionally, a beret or homburg or trilby hat. In today's rainbow and individualistic world, it is difficult to understand how comfortably conformist we were then. Most men settled for tweedy hacking jackets or old suit coats in sombre hues, while sons wore school blazers or jackets like their dad's. I haven't mentioned women in the crowd, because I don't remember seeing any.

As the latecomers squeezed in and the gates swung closed, the pre-match entertainment would begin. The star performer was a man with a tray of pastilles who appeared to almost as big a welcome as would greet the team. He was known as Old Herbal and had a catchphrase which had become a chant in its own right. 'Cough No More!' would be echoed by ten thousand throats when he started his vending cry. It is on such seeming inconsequential things that legends are built.

Old Herbal's skill was to be able to throw a packet of his pastilles from the cinder track to any part of the ground with unerring accuracy. The money would be handed down the terrace, the buyer would stick his hand up and the bag would sail through the air. Catching it cleanly earned a bonus cheer in the way of a crowd catch at a cricket ground.

Then the buzz would die down while the pre-match announcements were made on the tinny-sounding loud-speakers. It would be mostly team information and I particularly recall the ironic cheer when Blackpool were our guests and the news would come that Stanley Matthews would not be taking to the field. Whether or not it was true, it was always said that the great Stanley (later Sir Stanley) Matthews was, in local parlance 'trash' to play because he knew he would be targeted by a couple of the team's fearsome hard men. One was left back Harry Ferrier and the other was one of the most combatative players in the league. Jimmy Scoular's nickname was The Volcano, probably because of his incendiary eruptions if things didn't go his way. He was said to attack the man with the ball like a runaway coal wagon, and this was in the days when anything short of a broken limb was excused on the grounds of fair play.

At last the teams would enter the field of battle to a huge roar and cacophony of noise from rattles and hooters. Though they were local heroes most of the home players would be on not much more than the average wage and would end up taking a Portsmouth pub to make a living. But for these shining moments with the adoring roar of tens of thousands of fans ringing in their ears, they were kings.

At half time the marching bands of either the Royal Marines or the Portsmouth Fire Brigade would take to the field. The Marines were of course brilliant and the Fire Brigade rubbish and both would have to compete with a deafening rendition of the Pompey Chimes from the terraces. At the same time there would be a rush to the very basic urinals and the snack bar alongside. The cheese in the rolls was said to have been stolen from the mousetraps in the local orphanage, and the running joke about the meat pies was that visiting supporters thought that the green bits in them was cabbage.

Meanwhile, thousands of beer-swollen-bladdered men would be queuing for a place at the urinal trough and there would be some pungent odours abroad.

I still can't lift a mug of beef extract to my lips without recalling that exotic combination of the sharp tang of weak Bovril mixed with the all-pervading odour of ten thousand men relieving themselves in a place as dark and noisome as the Black Hole of Calcutta.

Printed in Great Britain
by Amazon

57155161R10131